RICHES
WITHOUT
RISK

RICHES
WITHOUT
RISK

A Worry-Free Investment Strategy for Good Times and Bad

GENE MACKEVICH

DODD, MEAD & COMPANY

NEW YORK

Library of Congress Cataloging-in-Publication Data

Mackevich, Gene, 1930–
    Riches without risk.

    Includes index.
    1. Investments.   2. Finance, Personal.   I. Title.
HG4521.M216   1986   332.024   86-2089
ISBN 0-396-08400-1
ISBN 0-396-08439-7 (pbk.)

CONTENTS

This book is dedicated to my parents, Ira and Alice, who have given me countless reasons to be grateful to them; to the other members of our financial planning team, including my wife, Barbara; my son, Jeffrey; my daughter, Marietta; Mary Beth, Denis, Christa, Mary, Ann, and Marci; and to my other daughters, Nancy and Beth, and to our clients for their trust and confidence.

ACKNOWLEDGMENTS

Although I assume personal responsibility for its contents, the technical advice provided in this book represents the accumulated knowledge and experience of our financial planning group. The most substantial contribution was that of my wife Barbara, a vice president of E. F. Hutton & Company and a Certified Financial Planner. My gratitude also goes to Phillip T. Drotning and Ricca Slone for their help in making complex material comprehensible for our readers.

Collectively, we have made every effort to provide accurate and authoritative information regarding the subject matter covered. Please note, however, that neither the publisher nor the author is engaged in providing legal or accounting advice. If legal, accounting, or other expert assistance is required, then the reader should solicit the services of competent professionals in these fields.

The publisher and the author specifically disclaim any personal liability for loss or risk incurred as a consequence of the use and application, either directly or indirectly, of any advice or information presented herein.

If you have additional questions regarding any of the information presented in this book, you may call the author at the National Investment Hotline number: (312) 435-4882. Please identify yourself as a reader of this book.

RICHES
WITHOUT
RISK

PART I

HOW TO PLAN YOUR WAY TO WEALTH

CHAPTER 1

HOW WELL ARE YOU MANAGING YOUR MONEY?

I n my role as an investment adviser, I meet and counsel thousands of men and women about their financial concerns. They attend and seek advice at the dozens of seminars I conduct each year or visit our offices to confer with me and my associates. Our clients include investors of all ages and degrees of sophistication. Some have substantial assets already; others are at the very beginning of the process of wealth accumulation. Yet, despite these differences, there is a common thread that brings them to me in the first place: *They are all smart enough to know that they should be doing a better job of managing their money.*

It's reasonable to assume that you share that conviction, or you wouldn't be reading this book. My purpose is to raise your comfort index by providing the information you need to maximize the yield from the assets you have today, protect those assets from the ravages of taxes and inflation, and enjoy your money, rather than worry about it.

Let's begin by determining what kind of money manager you are right now.

Many of the people we see are *accumulators*. They have learned the lesson of thrift, probably at their father's knee, and take comfort in saving money, but pay scant attention to what that money earns. They work energetically to earn money, sacrifice to save as much as possible, but overlook the opportunity to make their money work as hard as they do.

Some of these people learned something else from their fathers—FEAR! Daddy got burned in the Great Depression. He lost everything but his shirt and never trusted a financial institution for the rest of his life. He instilled in his kids what we call the "Depression syndrome." We see the results almost every day: men and women who are really misers, hoarding currency rather than putting it to work. They may have $50,000 or more, tucked away under their mattress waiting to be stolen, because they fear that banks or investments aren't "safe."

These are the people who avoid all risk and consistently make imprudent decisions to avoid it. They are too wary and suspicious to develop a sound relationship with a financial adviser. We see these people only when they are compelled by some dramatic event to face reality, as was the case with one elderly couple who distrusted everyone, including their long-standing attorney, and rejected all advice. They came to us after a year in which they paid $40,000 in income taxes, having decided that something in their attitude toward money wasn't right.

And then there are the *money-machines:* hard-working, intelligent men and women who are in the midst of spectacularly successful careers, but pay scant attention to their own financial goals. They know how to *make* money for themselves and their employers, but they don't know how to use their own money well. They haven't developed an investment philosophy, they haven't examined their tolerance for risk, they haven't explored the consequences of their investment choices. They don't know—in financial terms—where they are today or where they want to be tomorrow, so it is hardly surprising that their assets are not what they ought to be.

Occasionally, we see one of these people who must have

been born under a lucky star. We were visited one day by a man who was sent to us by another client. He had launched his own business years before, had worked hard at it, and had achieved remarkable success. Now, at age fifty-five, he had decided he wanted to retire and enjoy the fruits of his achievement.

When he walked into our office he had already sold his home, his business, and the building in which the business was operated. "I retired an hour ago," he said. "My wife and I have a new motor home, and we're leaving for Arizona as soon as I'm through here. I want you to invest this for me." With that, he handed me a check for $750,000. We persuaded him to work with us to develop a financial plan based on his future needs, and shortly thereafter he and his wife left for the Southwest. I haven't seen them since, but we have frequent telephone conversations to review his portfolio and make certain that it is appropriate to his own needs and plans. He's relieved of the need to manage his own money on a daily basis, but without sacrificing peace of mind.

Occasionally, such individuals can succeed without long-term planning, but they are clearly the exceptions. This client had done well, but that $750,000 check would have been much larger if he had established—years earlier—a sound financial plan. This couple is enjoying a comfortable retirement, and their assets have grown. They are enjoying their wealth today, and they are now developing a plan to preserve their assets for the benefit of their heirs.

Types of Investors

Too many Americans work a lifetime only to die broke after struggling through their retirement years. They never learned how to make their money work as hard as they did. They don't plan. They don't look at their financial future objectively and determine where they want to be five, ten, or twenty years from now, and what they must do to get there. They pay more income taxes than legally necessary. They don't understand the time value of money and the magic of compounding. They don't consider the true rate of inflation. Sometimes they put all their eggs in one basket, or too many eggs in the wrong basket. They ignore the inevitable—that the day will come when they no longer want to work, or are unable to do so.

Some are what I call *"no-brainers"*—casual folks who never give a moment's thought to managing their money and wake up too late, with their potential assets dissipated by thoughtless spending, taxes, and inflation. Obviously, you're not in this category, or you wouldn't be reading these words.

Others are *gamblers,* who succumb to a Las Vegas "get rich quick" mentality and fail to distinguish between investment and speculation. Lured by tales of fortunes made in high-risk areas such as the options or commodities markets, they enhance the fortunes of professionals who are full-time students of these markets, and they end up broke.

The *savers,* referred to earlier, may be the victims of ignorance as well as fear. They may be content with the pitifully small interest rates paid on passbook savings accounts because they are unaware of other safe investment opportunities that will pay them more.

The numbers in this category are diminishing because of the vast changes that have occurred within the financial industry in recent years. Competition has highlighted the vast range of investment opportunities now available that surpass traditional bank rates. Increasing numbers of savers are now aware that simply storing money in a passbook savings account makes no sense. Yet although their dollars may now be earning more than they once did, many potential investors are still not aware of the magnitude of their investable assets or of the opportunities afforded by the panoply of new financial products.

This is understandable, because of the complex array of investment choices that are available today. Only those with the time and inclination to become students of the financial markets can avoid becoming bewildered by the multiplicity of investment options, or frightened that they may diminish or even lose their assets in today's complex, fast-moving investment climate. Many of those I talk to are so wary of making an erroneous choice that they are unable to take any action at all.

These people then join the *procrastinators*, who probably constitute the largest category of all. They know they should act, but the moment to make that decision never seems to arrive. And not to decide, of course, is to decide.

Finally, I come to those whom I consider *investors*, those who are aware that they have many investment options and who have gone beyond certificates of deposit and money-market accounts. Too often, even in this more enlightened group, investors fail to develop—and stick to—an investment strategy that will maximize income and increase assets through *secure, high-yielding investments*. They have not designed an investment strategy that will enable them to survive and prosper through all the economic uncertainties that lie ahead.

A common failure within this group is a tendency to make spontaneous, haphazard decisions and take needless risks based on inadequate information or well-meant but bad advice. Too many investors make important decisions based on advice from friends, relatives, or business associates whose knowledge and judgment are no better than their own. Others rely uncritically on the guidance of so-called professionals: bankers, lawyers, accountants, stockbrokers, or insurance agents. Many of these "professionals" are ill-informed about the full range of investment opportunities, and frequently their advice is motivated by a self-serving interest in a particular form of investment. I've never known anyone who got rich by acting on bad advice!

In any field of endeavor, knowledge is power. In the pages that follow, I hope to give you knowledge, and thus the power, to control your own financial life and make the most of your assets in the years ahead.

Whom This Book Is For

The title of this book is *Riches Without Risk*. Presumably you bought it because you want to increase your wealth but don't want to risk losing the assets you already have. Those two words, *riches* and *risk,* are relative terms; they depend on your perspective, and there are degrees of both. Our definition of wealth increases as our income rises, and our definition of risk becomes less constraining as our assets give us more latitude to expose ourselves to it. What you may expect, if you accept the guidance I will try to provide, is a steady increase in your assets and little risk of losing the assets that are already yours.

This book is not for the relative handful of semiprofessional investors who have the time and the knowledge to consider investing a major occupation. Nor is it intended only for the wealthy. Rather, it is for those with less expertise who probably are not wealthy yet—those who want to use their assets and their earning power to gain the comfort and security that comes with increased wealth. It is for those who have accumulated some investable assets—in any amount—and are ready to develop a formal financial plan that will put their income to work and maximize the growth of the assets they invest. This group includes those who need assistance the most: middle-income families who are earning $25,000 to $75,000 a year and who have watched their ability to accumulate wealth pinched by rising costs and taxes. Everyone can benefit from understanding how to plan and by learning how to use low-risk investments to convert their plan to reality.

This book has a very simple objective: to help you increase your assets by maximizing earnings, avoiding income taxes, and guarding against the ravages of inflation—without significant risk of loss of capital. It will explore the mysteries of investing, in layman's terms, and reveal the safest ways for you to put your money to work. In essence, its purpose is to help you find your way through the investment jungle by giving you a road map for self-help.

Meanwhile, I want to try to help you lighten up your attitude toward money. Financial concerns dominate too many lives. They destroy sleep and even marriages. Once you have mastered the concepts in this book you can take control of your financial future, stop worrying about it, and free your energy for other pursuits. There is nothing rewarding about preoccupation with money for money's sake. The reward you'll get from thoughtful financial planning is the freedom to do what you want with your life.

Planning an Investment Strategy

It must be clear by now that my purpose is to make you think like a *planner*. If you are a *gambler* or a *no-brainer*, I can't help you unless you change your attitude, but chances are if you are in either of those categories you wouldn't be reading this book. But if you are now a saver, I will help you to become an investor. If you are already an investor, I want you to become a planner. I want to help every reader move down the path toward wealth. Financial planning is the one and only vehicle that will enable you to manage your finances wisely. Sound planning is not specific to any financial product; nor is its usefulness limited to tax or retirement or estate-planning purposes. It involves dispassionate evaluation of your stage of life, your overall financial resources, your present and prospective income, and your tolerance for risk. It requires that you identify potential problems, analyze current and foreseeable future needs, and define your goals and set measurable objectives. It means understanding and exploring investment options, and developing and adhering to a budget and an overall financial strategy. It means taking action to reduce your tax burden and to build and preserve your capital.

The plan you develop will not be cast in concrete. You must be prepared and willing to update it as your circumstances change. It must be a plan you can apply and live with.

CHAPTER 2

DEVELOPING A SOUND FINANCIAL PLAN

In some societies the only way to become rich is to be born that way. Happily, in this land of opportunity, the prospect of wealth is available to everyone. We are surrounded by examples of wealth derived from diligence, hard work, and sound financial planning. Some people are just lucky, of course, but planners make their own luck, and, by planning, they can make themselves rich.

Planners know how much they're worth. In my experience, most people don't. Most of my clients, after they have identified their assets, are astonished to discover that they are wealthier than they thought.

Planners know their cash-flow requirements and their anticipated future needs for funds for the education of their children, parental support, their own retirement, or other milestones in their lives. They do not let future financial needs take them by surprise.

Planners can make maximum use of their assets because they have clearly understood investment objectives, geared to their own unique situation and personal needs. They develop sound investment strategies that will enable them to meet their objectives while protecting their assets from erosion by inflation and avoidable tax liabilities. With this strategy, planners can make investment choices appropriate to their individual requirements and to current economic and market conditions.

Planners know that timing is everything, and they continuously monitor the potential of alternative investment categories (e.g., stocks vs. bonds vs. gold), investment groups within those categories (e.g., oil vs. high tech vs. biogenetics), and individual companies within those groups (e.g., Mobil vs. Texaco vs. Amoco). They use their own research, coupled with that of their investment advisers or financial planners, to determine when to buy and when to sell.

Planners don't put all their eggs in one basket. They diversify their holdings so that a decline in the value of one investment will be offset by increases in others. They avoid the risks of greed and are willing to settle for a small profit to avoid the threat of a large loss. They don't let ego restrain them from taking a loss when it is appropriate and wise to do so. Yet they have the savvy to spot investments with the potential for major appreciation, and the patience and guts to await the payoff.

Planning is the essence of truly sophisticated investing, the element that enables you to take control of your money and your life—now and in the future. With planning, every desirable outcome of money management is possible, from minimizing tax liability to protecting assets against inflation. Without planning, none of these outcomes is certain, or even likely.

The Costs of Failure to Plan

The virtues of planning are so obvious that it is astonishing how low a priority it has in most American households. Many families who strive faithfully to follow a household budget believe that this is a financial plan. Certainly, a realistic household budget is an essential ingredient, but it is not a financial plan.

When I ask new clients why they have neglected developing a plan of their own, I get a variety of responses. Many believe that their affairs are already in good order. Others tell me they didn't believe that their assets or income merited a plan. Most of them, however, acknowledge rather sheepishly that they had realized for some time that their financial situation needed attention. Like a dreaded trip to the dentist, they kept putting it off until tomorrow, and tomorrow never came.

If you're in that category, take heart. It is never too late to plan. Take comfort in the fact that many families, even some of the most affluent, have glaring weak spots in their financial management. Most common are hit-or-miss investing, excessive outlays for life insurance, inadequate disability and household insurance, and failure to look ahead—evidenced most often by the absence of an up-to-date will.

Many families whose assets and income merit the help of a professional financial counselor are deterred from seeking help by what they perceive as the high cost of planning assistance. They don't know that much of this cost can be offset by tax deductions and that failure to plan is costing them far more.

These costs are not limited to needlessly high income taxes. Forward-looking planners are concerned about gift and real estate taxes as well. They begin early to consider the future welfare of their heirs. If they own all or a large portion of a closely held business, they are aware that failure to plan for its future disposition can cause severe hardship in the event of death, disability, or retirement. Perhaps the greatest cost of failure to plan is purely personal: It diminishes your ability to achieve your objectives in life.

It is apparent from the questions asked at my seminars that many people who want professional help are embarrassed about seeking it because their assets are not in the megabuck range. They needn't be, because all professional financial advisers who are worth consulting welcome clients who are at every rung on the financial ladder. Planners plan ahead, too, and they know that while you may not be affluent today, they can help make you wealthy tomorrow.

It is obvious, if you think about it, that less affluent people may actually need financial planning the most, because each dollar of increased income or capital means relatively more to them. Even if a potential client has only a few thousand dollars to invest, I am interested in his account. I learned long ago that a serious young investor of limited means, but initiative and desire to use that money wisely, will become a larger investor as the years go by.

Goals: A Lifetime Perspective

The first questions I ask someone who comes to me for financial help are: What are your goals in life? Where do you want to be a year from now, five years, ten, when you finally retire? The questions are provocative. I want to draw answers out. A majority of clients of this stage have never even considered their financial situation in such definitive terms, and others offer only the vaguest of replies.

To begin planning effectively, you must ask yourself three basic questions: Where am I now? Where do I want to go? How can I get there? As you ponder your replies, bear in mind that there are three critical phases in your financial life cycle. They are *wealth accumulation, wealth preservation,* and *wealth distribution.* Their importance will alter as you move through life, but from the outset you must keep all of them in mind.

Within those phases are some essential elements that must always be considered:

1. Adequate liquid reserves to tide you over during periods of unemployment, major property or liability losses, or other emergencies

2. Adequate medical, disability, and life insurance protection
3. Preparation for the future education needs of your children
4. Planning for financial independence upon retirement
5. Preservation and distribution of your estate

Let's take a closer look at each of the life-cycle phases:

Building wealth should be the overarching financial objective of young singles and married couples, or anyone at any age who has not begun building wealth up to now. The most promising strategy is a firm decision to "pay yourself first," taking your savings share off the top of every paycheck, rather than paying your bills, going on a shopping spree, and then saving what is left. Unless your decision on how much you will regularly save is inviolate, the odds are that *there won't be anything left.* Ten percent of salary is a reasonable initial goal for most young people, but as your income increases, your savings, not just your standard of living, should also increase. If your employer offers a company savings plan, participate to the maximum extent. Many companies match the amount you save, and their contribution, as well as earned interest and dividends, are tax-deferred.

A consistent savings plan will build a reserve for emergencies and ultimately will provide your first nest egg of investable assets. It may not seem so at the outset, but saving will become a rewarding experience, not a painful one. You can make it more so, early on, by rewarding yourself with a vacation or some other pleasant fling. Don't be too generous with yourself, however, for you must regard your savings as absolutely serious money.

Invest the maximum that is allowed in an IRA or Keogh for retirement, and the remainder in other prudent investments that will help you to reach your long-term goals. I am constantly perplexed by the failure of so many people to take advantage of the tax benefits available in these retirement-savings mechanisms, and their failure to invest the funds wisely. Too many IRAs are languishing in low-yield CDs.

I also advise my younger clients, whose responsibilities to others are limited, to experiment with a limited amount of money that they feel they can comfortably afford to risk. Try a few aggressive investments with a high growth potential, but do it while you can safely endure some risk of capital loss.

As a young couple begins having children, although their income may be increasing, expenses are likely to increase at a more rapid rate. Security for your dependents becomes critical, and steps must be taken to assure it. Young parents, while they're still changing diapers, should begin considering actions that will provide for their child's education in future years. College costs are soaring, and it makes sense to make modest sacrifices now, rather than traumatic ones later, to provide for these educational needs.

During these years, adequate life, health, and disability insurance should also be maintained, but here a word of caution is in order. Whole-life insurance, which combines protection and savings, is a foolish way to invest. Buy term insurance to protect your children while they are still dependent on you and curtail that coverage as the need diminishes.

Don't overlook the importance of your *rate* of investment—the actual amounts you faithfully put aside. Because of compounding, your rate of investment is at least as important as your rate of return. When you get a salary increase, use as much of it as possible to build up your assets. Then, as your family income rises into the higher tax brackets, consider tax-advantaged investments that enable you to defer taxes and have the potential for capital gains.

The recently divorced and widowed are confronted with the most difficult concerns. If they have not been employed, they often find that they lack the skills and experience to provide for themselves. Meanwhile, they lack sophistication in financial management, and often are the victims of very bad advice. I have specialized in counseling women in this category, and even wrote a book to try to help them. Too often they are victimized in such matters as coverage under the deceased provider's group health insurance, claims against his retirement plan, and the cash value and equity buildup in his life insurance policies. Many who are divorced fail to consider the tax consequences of the settlement they reach. Frequently, after a bitter and protracted battle over division of the family's assets, and provisions regarding alimony and child support, the only winner is the IRS.

By midlife, your financial needs and opportunities will probably undergo a significant change. Your children will have their college diplomas and be self-supporting and off on their own. Your home mortgage will be no more than an unpleasant memory, and your insurance needs and household expenses will diminish. You will have reached the point when you can begin providing exclusively for yourself.

The preretirement years, beginning in one's mid-fifties, are the peak earning years in most of our careers. With your other obligations out of the way, they provide the opportunity for you to build the assets that will assure your ability to retire in comfort and with dignity when your working years are over. Your psychological tolerance for risk will be reduced, and tax planning and tax avoidance will assume increased importance.

This is when the goal of *wealth preservation* comes into play. You want to accumulate all the money you can and protect the assets you already have. You'll place increased emphasis on diversification of investments. You will begin to plan how you will withdraw assets from pension funds, IRAs, or Keogh accounts. You'll take a hard look at your health insurance coverage, particularly if you plan to retire before you reach age 65. You may no longer be covered by your former employer and yet not be eligible for Medicare. If you haven't already done so, this is also the time to begin planning for *wealth distribution:* how you will arrange for the disposition of your assets when, inevitably, you die.

During your retirement years, security and wealth-distribution considerations become paramount. If you planned carefully and invested shrewdly when you were younger, your retirement income may equal or even exceed that of your working years. Your expenses will be reduced, and you can look forward to comfort and security for the remainder of your years.

On the other hand, maybe you can't. As many have discovered to their sorrow, just when they thought their worries were over inflation reared its ugly head. It eroded the value of their fixed income and cost them both the comfort and the dignity they thought they had achieved. The strategies you learned in building your wealth will now be required to keep it from slipping away. And, unless you keep abreast of the tax laws, update your estate plan when necessary, and judiciously employ gifts and trust to protect your assets, Uncle Sam, not your heirs, may be the principal beneficiary of all the thought and effort you have expended over the years.

As this discussion illustrates, your broad objectives will evolve logically over time. Regard everything you do with money as investment, whether the reward is immediate self-gratification or comfort and security in later years. Evaluating this tradeoff and making rational, conscious choices is the beginning of sound financial management.

Understanding Investment Risk

Developing an appropriate investment strategy requires that you determine your tolerance for risk. The element of risk in investing, as in life, is almost always there, but it is possible to temper the degree of risk or to trade one type of risk for another that is more acceptable to you.

The most basic risk, and the one most frightening to most investors, is the risk of loss of capital. Many of those who come to me for financial advice are unaware of at least six other risks that should also concern them. They are:

Illiquidity risk: The absence of a market for your investment when you are compelled to sell. Collectibles and real estate are prime examples.

Interest-rate risk: The degree of volatility in interest rates, which can affect everything from the present value and saleability of bonds to the certainty of future streams of income.

Corporate or business risk: The risk of having all your assets in a single company or industry that may suffer from technological obsolescence, loss of market share, mismanagement, or bankruptcy.

Inadequate diversification risk: The risk of investing your assets in too few investments, or in a single type of investment, like bonds or stocks. Risk avoidance requires a balanced portfolio that will hedge effectively against the vicissitudes of the market.

Time risk: Building wealth is a function of the amount invested and the rate of return, but *time* is an essential factor, too. You must have the patience to wait until your investment strategy pays off. But you must also know when to act decisively, and when to take a loss. Unless you monitor your investments, and pay close attention to the investment climate, you won't be able to do either one.

Inflation: The real rate of return on the funds you have invested is profoundly affected by the inflation rate.

I've had clients who came to me delighted with a 9-percent yield on their certificates of deposit at a time when the inflation rate was 15 percent. They didn't realize that their assets were not increasing; they were being eroded at the rate of 6 percent a year!

If your greatest fear is loss of capital, you can design an investment portfolio that will avoid that risk, but not without exposing yourself to one or more of the others. Most of the risky investment categories are well known and widely used, common stocks being the prime example. Indeed, many of my new clients fail to recognize the existence of any forms of investment other than certificates of deposit, bonds, and common stocks. They are unaware that the accelerated pace of change in the financial industry has created many new opportunities to invest in more predictable, high-yielding, and low-risk investments.

Your risk tolerance should dictate your investment portfolio, for it is folly to try to increase your wealth if you are condemned to worry yourself sick while you're doing it. A defensive or conservative portfolio would include a relatively high proportion of cash or cash equivalents like Treasury bills, money-market funds, and bank certificates of deposit; blue-chip stocks paying high dividends; income-producing real estate; and perhaps some gold coins or gold mutual funds. An aggressive investor, with funds he can comfortably afford to risk, might choose emerging growth stocks, leveraged real estate, or multiple-write-off tax shelters.

I believe that the bulk of any investor's money is too serious for high-risk investments like aggressive common stocks. A prudent investor will take care of the basics first, meeting expenses, establishing a reserve fund for emergencies, and providing for foreseeable events like education or retirement with IRAs or Keoghs. That's what I call "untouchable money." "Serious money" goes into other safe investments, which I will discuss in detail. Only "fun money" that you can afford to lose should go into investments with a very high level of risk.

Basically, my advice to most of my clients is to avoid any investment that has unnecessary risk. Beyond that, there are ways to reduce the risks of some forms of investments—common stocks, for example—which I will discuss later in this book.

Why avoid high-risk investments? First, the obvious. You don't want the capital you have worked so diligently to accumulate to disappear. Second, you can't plan effectively if the plan is based on risky investments, and planning and profit are what this book is all about. It is a widely held fallacy that the greater the risk, the greater the reward. In fact, if you consider preservation of capital as well as rate of return, it is usually the other way around.

Safety and high returns can be compatible. The most profitable investment opportunities for the past five years have also been the most secure. Risk avoidance guarantees the safety of your capital and protects you against inflation. These investments are predictable, allowing you to plan effectively. They are winners. They are where 90 percent of all investors belong with 90 percent of their money. *And they probably are not what you think they are!*

When you learn, through planning, to use these investments to your advantage, you can enjoy the benefits of psychological comfort, financial security, and the rewarding life that money can provide. *Riches without risk*—that's what planning will give to you.

The Investment Pyramid

It has been observed that, while there is no investment for all seasons, there is a season for all investments. Investments that are appropriate at one point in time may be those to avoid at another. Interest rates, changes in the money supply, alterations in your tolerance for risk as you move through the life cycle, and even the magnitude of your investable assets may cause you to alter your investment policies.

A useful device to help you develop an investment strategy, and modify it as the need arises, is the investment pyramid illustrated on the facing page. The pyramid is structured primarily according to the degree of risk of loss of capital. The most dangerous and least liquid investments are at the top, where the pyramid narrows to a point—a graphic warning that only a small portion of your assets (if any) belongs here. A venture into this area is akin to a trip to Las Vegas or Atlantic City. There is no guaranteed safety of principal, and even the earnings are speculative, rather than assured. True—just as at the roulette wheel—there is the prospect that you may make a killing, but there is an even greater prospect that you may sustain a huge loss. Only those with a sound investment portfolio in place, and "fun money" to play with, should even consider investments of this type. Examples, discussed more thoroughly elsewhere in this book, include commodity futures, high-risk tax shelters, and even common stocks.

The broad base of the pyramid, which should also form

the base of your investment portfolio, includes the least risky and most liquid investment opportunities. It includes so-called defensive investments such as cash and cash equivalents, Treasury bills, and common stocks protected by put options that will defend against substantial loss. In between are other conservative investments that include fixed annuities, bond funds, and unit trusts.

The pyramid illustrates the importance of building a firm foundation that will assure your ability to take care of your primary financial needs and venture into more speculative investments only when that base is firmly in place. A widely used rule of thumb is that 80 percent of your funds should be defensively or conservatively invested when the economic outlook is threatening, but only 50 percent or less when the outlook improves. I favor an even less aggressive

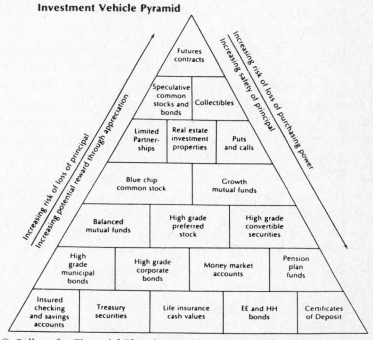

Investment Vehicle Pyramid

© College for Financial Planning. 1983   Reprinted with permission approach, believing that low-risk, conservative investing is the wisest course for most investors most of the time. I distrust pat formulas such as this because they fail to incorporate key factors such as individual risk tolerance and the investor's stage in the life cycle.

Personal Financial Planning

Personal financial planning is the process of developing and implementing a thoughtful, coordinated plan to achieve all of your overall financial objectives. If you focus on your general and specific financial objectives, your investment decisions will be more rational and will make sense for you and for your family. Without a plan you risk becoming confused by the enticing array of financial products, and the possibility that you may make ad hoc decisions to purchase particular instruments simply because a friend or broker recommends them. Equally important, knowing your objectives and risk tolerance permits you to develop investment policies: for example, what percentage of your portfolio (if any) should go into fixed-dollar securities like bonds, and what proportion into equity investments like stocks.

If you are in the first stage of the life cycle, just beginning the process of wealth accumulation and considering for the first time your investment alternatives, you can use the information in this book to develop your own financial plan. As you move through life, and your available assets become more substantial, you may wish to fortify your own knowledge with advice from one or more professionals who are specialists in various fields. Many of my more affluent clients have adopted a sort of systems approach to planning and meeting their financial goals. They have consulted their attorneys, accountants, trust officers, insurance agents, and stockbrokers in order to develop a cohesive plan that will serve them, not any of the individual specialists. They absorb all of the available advice but, after hearing it, reserve to themselves the final decision regarding which of the advice should be rejected and which elements should be incorporated into their financial plan.

The Planning Process

No two financial plans will be exactly alike; nor should they be, because in one or more areas, every family's needs are unique. Each of us has different goals, available resources, family requirements, and psychological needs. Moreover, we begin the planning effort at different points in the life cycle. I have clients who are still in high school, and others who didn't come to me until after they retired at age 65.

Nevertheless, certain elements are consistent in every effort to develop a financial plan. Inevitably, the process must begin with *analysis*. The purpose of the analysis is to answer the question: Where am I now? Only with that information as the base can you plan how to get where you want to go.

I won't mislead you by allowing you to believe that analysis is an easy task that you can almost perform off the top of your head. If you do it thoroughly, you can expect to do some very hard work.

First, you must gather a mind-boggling array of information about all aspects of your present financial situation and your financial history up to now. This will include your available cash, your insurance policies, your retirement, disability, and medical benefits, your past income tax records, any existing wills and trusts, and the specifics of the assets you presently have invested. A detailed list of the information you will need is included on pages 26–27.

Having assembled these data, you can prepare (or have your financial planner prepare) your personal financial statements. Of these, the most crucial is your personal balance sheet. This will tell you what you own (your assets) and what you owe (your liabilities), from which you can determine your net worth. Don't be surprised to discover that your net worth exceeds your expectations.

You should also prepare a personal income statement that reveals your earned and investment income; a cash-flow statement that shows the sources and timing of your cash receipts; and a household budget that incorporates your household and personal expenses and your savings goals.

Gathering all of this information will be a difficult and frustrating task, but it is not a chore you can readily delegate to someone else. Depending on the complexity of your individual financial situation, it may require tremendous discipline to get it done. It is essential, however, to financial planning, and may have the added value of revealing how inadequate your financial management has been and what that has cost you in years past.

Financial Records

You will need to assemble these records:

Checking and savings accounts: banks, account numbers, balances

Time deposits: banks, account numbers, maturity dates, interest rates

Money-market funds: name, number of shares, current value

Life insurance policies: policy numbers, beneficiaries, current cash value

Employee benefits: when vested, estimated value at retirement

Residence: location of deeds, estimated current value, mortgage balance

Liabilities: credit card balances, other account balances, installment loans, outstanding personal or

commercial notes, alimony and child support obligations

*Attorney, accountant, executor, trustee, stockbroker, in-
surance agents:* names, addresses, phone numbers

State and federal income tax records

Keogh plans and IRAs: where invested, account
numbers, current value

Wills and trusts: copies, when last updated

Investment property: purchase date, purchase price,
current market value

Hard assets (gold, gems, etc.): purchase date, price,
estimated current market value

Your financial records will enable you to review your
assets and liabilities, determine your net worth, and compute your investable assets and working capital. After establishing a liquid reserve to support your household for
three to six months in the event of an emergency, you now
know how much is available for investment to meet other
goals.

Setting Investment Priorities

Most of my clients, when they have completed this ar-
duous chore, are delighted to find that they are in better
financial shape than they thought they were. That's when
the fun begins for them, and so will it be with you as well.
You are now in a position to determine the first priorities
among your objectives and decide on the distribution of
your assets among these priorities. Then analyze your present position in relation to your objectives. Here are the sort
of questions you should think about:

Is your liquid contingency reserve adequate to
handle emergencies?

If there is a shortfall, how can it be made up?

What are your household and personal expenses, and how much can you set aside from each paycheck to increase your wealth?

If this seems inadequate, can you reduce some elements of expense to make greater savings possible?

What kind of equity buildup do various investment alternatives offer?

The remainder of this book will familiarize you with some of these alternatives and enable you to make informed choices among them, depending on your priorities and needs.

Don't be afraid to work with professional counselors in pursuit of a financial game plan that is right for you. You will benefit if you seek more than one opinion or request more than one set of options, even though some of the advice you receive may be in conflict. Ultimately, you will rely on your own instincts and knowledge to determine the plan that is most comfortable for you.

Most of my clients find it helpful to set some intermediate benchmarks or targets as they develop their plan. There is so much riding on it that it may seem to be an impossibly formidable task. You may find the process more manageable if you approach it a step at a time.

Once your financial plan has been developed to your satisfaction, it is time to act. Some investors are frightened by the decisions they must make, but they shouldn't be. Any decision is better than no decision, and those you make are certain to be more prudent than the ones you would have to make if you had no plan at all.

Finally, develop a schedule for periodic review and revision of your plan. Circumstances change. So do objectives.

The effort you have expended will lose its value if you fail to have your plan keep up with the times!

How to Select a Financial Planner

Many readers will feel that they need some help to get through the planning process. If you are one of them, give serious consideration to engaging a financial planner.

Don't settle for a random name picked from the Yellow Pages. All it takes to be listed there is the price of the ad. Select a planner as carefully as you would a doctor when your life is at stake. When you make this choice your financial life is, indeed, at stake.

Look for a qualified financial planner with ample experience, one whom a stable of knowledgeable and affluent clients has already learned to trust. He should be a well-informed generalist, but he cannot be expected to be an expert on every financial product. He should, therefore, have continuing access to such experts and be affiliated with a reputable broker-dealer. While you will want to consult specialists in some forms of investment, your planner should not be solely a stockbroker or a specialist himself. He may be consciously or unconsciously prejudiced in favor of financial products in which he has a personal financial stake.

If you have a tax accountant or attorney, he may be able to refer you to one or more financial planners whom he considers competent. You may also obtain recommendations from friends who are already using planning services.

Your choice of a financial planner is crucial, so it is vital that you find a financial planner you trust. You may wish to interview more than one before you make a final decision. Most planners will offer an initial exploratory consultation free of charge. Use this time to learn all you can about the planner's experience, education and training, and personality characteristics. If you encounter a planner who has a ready solution to your problems before examining the details of your individual financial situation, scratch him from your list. You don't want pat answers. You need sound advice, based on a thorough knowledge of your unique, individual needs.

Competent planners should welcome your inquiries and provide you with an estimate of their fees and an accounting of the commission they will receive on products they will recommend. Your choice should be governed by your own evaluation of the individual planners whom you interview. Ultimately, it will probably be an intuitive choice, based on the individual's credentials, your sense of his integrity, and, most of all, your level of comfort in dealing with him.

What Your Financial Planner Should Do for You

Ideally, the planner you select should survey your entire financial situation: current cash flow, budget, net worth, investments, savings, taxes, insurance, retirement, and estate arrangements. All these elements must be shaped into a program uniquely designed to achieve your particular goals.

The planner works with information from interviews and, most of all, from a very detailed questionnaire that could take you several hours to complete. As I have already warned, collecting and organizing the required information and spelling out your goals is a tough job. Whether you have a planner or not, it is not one that you can escape or shift to someone else.

Finally, your planner must help you carry out your plan with specific suggestions. Any recommendations you get should not favor excessively the products or services the planner happens to sell, or those that yield the highest commission for him.

Since you must provide the basic information anyway, why not do your own plan? You could, incorporating the information in this book, but I don't advise it because of the risks inherent in the "do-it-yourself" approach.

For example, objective analysis of your financial situation and alternatives by a competent professional planner may reveal hazards and opportunities that would not have been apparent to you. Moreover, the greater your income and investment portfolio, the greater the chance that you will benefit from sophisticated advice, particularly on taxes, retirement options, and estate planning. Those in the upper-income brackets typically utilize professionals for legal, tax, and investment advice, but many need a professional planner to coordinate the advice into a cohesive strategy.

Financial planning is essential for everyone who is serious about using money productively and building for the future. It's not about any particular financial product; nor is it only for tax or estate-planning purposes.

A financial planner works with your accountant and attorney, but has a different role: helping you to plan a secure and productive financial strategy. He will help you get organized, identify problems, define goals, set measurable objectives, and then identify, coordinate, and invest your resources to assure maximum earnings and asset growth. He will, in short, help you to create a plan that you can apply and live with.

Questions to Ask the Planner You Select

You have employed a financial planner and supplied him with all of the data he requested, and he has now presented you with a financial plan. You have been comfortable with him throughout the process and you believe that you are getting sound advice. But how can you be sure? Here are some questions you might ask to test the quality of his work:

1. *How does this plan differ from others you have designed?*
A sound financial plan should be unique, designed to fit

the individual circumstances of the individual for whom it was produced. Your planner should be able to relate his recommendations to the details of your personal financial situation and the information he has gleaned from you about your own objectives and needs. If he can't do that, be suspicious, for the needs the plan meets may be his own and not yours.

2. *Does this plan give me ample liquidity to deal with emergencies if they arise?*

As a rule of thumb, you should maintain liquid assets sufficient to cover your expenses for a three-month period if your income should, for some reason, cease.

3. *Is the portfolio you propose appropriately diversified?*

A conscientious planner should balance your assets among different investments so your total return will be reasonably stable and the total asset value secure, despite market or interest-rate fluctuations. Unless special circumstances prevail, no single investment should exceed 50 percent of the total portfolio, but your plan also should not read like a shopping list of every known investment product.

4. *What annual returns can I expect on the portfolio you recommend?*

You will be doing well if your net return (after taxes) consistently outpaces inflation by 3 or 5 percent a year. The bottom line is not the rate of interest or dividends paid on an investment, but what you have left after your income taxes are paid.

5. *Have you exercised due diligence on the products you recommend?*

Financial advisers are required to make reasonable efforts to determine that the products they recommend are both fiscally and legally sound. Your planner should, for example, be knowledgeable about the general partner's record in any tax-sheltering limited partnership. Be aware that most planners, including those who work for institutions, rely entirely on research provided by broker-dealers who supply products and conduct the required investigations. Ask your planner to summarize the nature of this research and tell you why he's satisfied that it is accurate.

6. *Does the portfolio you recommend allow sufficient flexibility to adapt to substantial changes in the investment climate?*

The value and yield of various forms of investment can shift radically with changes in the inflation rate, interest rates, and other factors. An ideal portfolio should maximize your ability to shift from one investment category to another, with minimum penalty, if circumstances warrant it.

7. *How can I monitor whether the plan you propose is achieving its goals?*

Your planner should agree to provide you with a periodic report on the status of the investments in your portfolio and recommend changes if they are desirable.

8. *Will this plan help me to realize my retirement goals?*

Depending on your age at the time your plan is devised, your portfolio may not be appropriate to your requirements during the decade prior to retirement. When that period arrives, your portfolio should be sufficiently flexible so that it can be altered to serve your emerging needs. At that time, your planner should be able to estimate the income you can expect from Social Security, your IRA or Keogh plan, company-pension and tax-deferred savings plans, and your investment portfolio. He should then develop a schedule for gradually shifting your priorities in favor of capital preservation and increased income.

PART II

INVESTMENT OPPORTUNITIES: LOOKING AT RISK

CHAPTER 3

NONINVESTMENT INVESTMENTS

A Chicago savings and loan institution opened a new branch office several years ago and gave premiums (toasters, television sets, etc.) to those who opened new accounts. An elderly lady, not too sophisticated but independent and stubborn, put a very large sum of money—over $100,000—in the S & L. The institution subsequently went into bankruptcy, and the lady did not get her money back for over a year. Although she believed, as most depositors do, that the Federal Savings and Loan Insurance Corporation (FSLIC) would return her deposits immediately, she got nothing but an IOU. She had no access to the funds she had deposited and earned no interest on them. The funds were not returned to her until fourteen months had passed.

Her story is a tragic one, but the next chapter is even more so. The savings and loan went through a Chapter 11 reorganization and reopened. It is doing business again, but it is undercapitalized, on shaky ground, and on the state and federal lists of institutions in trouble. Nevertheless, the lady returned to the S & L and redeposited her money. This time she got a coffee pot!

This lady is a classic example, although admittedly an extreme one, of the *saver* mentality. To her credit, she is wise enough to appreciate the virtues of thrift, but she has refused for fifty years to contemplate the possibility that deposits in a regulated financial institution may not be the safest and wisest investments that she can possibly make. Despite my best efforts and her own experience to the contrary, I still haven't been able to convince her otherwise.

Many thrifty and well-intentioned people invest by habit. Those who confine their assets to the money market, and reject all other investment options, are what I call *savers*. They are comfortable only with the flexibility and liquidity of cash (or cash equivalents) or short-term government-backed securities.

The High Cost of the Saver's Mentality

While everyone needs adequate funds in liquid form for daily expenses and emergency purposes, such assets should always constitute a carefully controlled and monitored proportion of one's total portfolio. In today's investment climate, it is generally inexcusable to hold all of your assets in cash or cash equivalents. Yet millions of savers do it, at great expense to themselves.

Some of these savers are simply lazy; others are uninformed. But I believe that the majority are so fearful of loss of capital that they fail to protect against interest-rate risk, market risk, and inflation risk, and continue to pay more income taxes then they should. They ignore the opportunities for true capital growth that are available to them, while their assets are eaten away by taxes and inflation.

In many cases, those in this category began a forced savings plan when they were young, on the theory that if they didn't see the money they wouldn't spend it. At the outset, this theory probably had psychological validity, but once they had accumulated sufficient liquid assets to deal with expenses and emergencies, it ceased to make economic sense.

The earnings were too low, the inflation penalties too high, and the tax bite too large.

The person with this kind of mind-set also pays in other ways. First, with his principal at substantial risk (inflation risk), his security may be more fancied than real. Second, he is sacrificing opportunities for greater capital appreciation or higher interest from other forms of investment without a corresponding increase in capital risk.

Many of the readers of this book undoubtedly will be savers. If you are among them, I hope you will open your mind about managing your money and begin to think like an investor. You will, of course, want to maintain some funds in cash and cash equivalents, and even to move funds out of other investments temporarily, when market and economic conditions make it prudent to do so. However, this action should be the consequence of a rational decision, not the continuation of a lifelong habit, and you should make an informed choice among the financial institutions and types of accounts that are available to you.

Let's examine some of these accounts and institutions. They are not all alike, or as alike as they once were, because of deregulation and the tremendous upheavals in the financial-service industry in recent years.

Banks and Savings and Loan Institutions

Most savers seems to have unshakable faith in the safety of their deposits in conventional savings institutions. This confidence is reinforced by advertising that stresses "insured deposits" and even by the architecture of many banks and S & Ls. Savers walk by their bank and take comfort in the belief that their savings are resting securely behind those Grecian pillars and protected by Uncle Sam.

For those who were paying attention, that image suffered a severe jolt when one of the world's largest banks, the Continental Illinois Bank and Trust Company of Chicago, got in so much trouble that it had to be bailed out by the Federal Deposit Insurance Corporation. On the heels of that crisis came the debacle of insolvent savings and loans in Ohio and Maryland, causing depositors to lose access to their money when government officials forced these institutions to close their doors. These savings and loans were not federally insured.

The savings instruments offered by these institutions are not of adequate investment quality and some of them are not even appropriate for storing cash. The worst offender is the traditional passbook savings account, which still pays as little as 5¼ percent. It seems almost inconceivable that billions of dollars remain in passbook savings accounts around the nation, generating profits for the banking institution that could be earned by the depositors.

NOW checking accounts are almost as bad. SuperNOW accounts are somewhat more productive, as are money-market accounts, depending on the minimum-deposit requirements and the penalties for falling below the minimum average balance that is required. Beware, also, of the advertised interest rates paid on these accounts. The true interest is a function of the frequency of compounding; that is, whether the interest earned is calculated daily, monthly, or over an even longer period.

It is also important to compare checking-account fees charged by various savings institutions. Some of the service charges and penalties are unconscionable, so shop around and make the best deal you can. But remember, always, that you are shortchanging yourself when you keep a dollar more in a checking account than what you need to pay current bills.

Although the troubled Ohio and Maryland S & Ls were

insured by agencies other than the FSLIC, their insolvency focused attention on the problems of other S & Ls throughout the United States, most of which *are* federally insured.

S & Ls, in general, have been having difficulties for several years. When interest rates soared to double digits, they were paying as much as 11 or 12 percent on incoming deposits while they had billions in mortgages on their books at only 7 or 8 percent. Their assets dwindled because of the negative cash flow. Curiously, the recession of the early 1980s actually helped these financial institutions stay afloat. The large number of mortgage foreclosures enabled them to liquidate unprofitable loans and write new ones at higher rates.

The fine print of many S & L passbooks says "not payable on demand." Some S & Ls have actually given their depositors script or IOUs because their assets were insufficient to sustain their operating losses. Their depositors discovered, to their sorrow, that their state-chartered S & L, although insured, was not federally insured, and that the state insurance fund was exhausted.

Even federal insurance is not all that depositors believe it to be. One of the most frightening of potential calamities stems from the fact that the FSLIC has reserves of less than 2 percent of the funds deposited at a time when countless institutions are on the regulators' "trouble" list. If there were a run on federally insured S & Ls—not improbable given the number of forced mergers already underway—I hate to think about the consequences.

Bank Certificates of Deposit

Certificates of deposit have better yields than savings accounts if they are left on deposit for a fixed period, but they still leave you vulnerable to the twin investment cancers—

taxes and inflation. For example, the actual return on a 3-year $10,000 CD paying 10 percent interest is not what, at first glance, it appears to be.

Even using a relatively low hypothetical inflation rate of 6 percent, an investor in a 40-percent bracket has virtually no increase in real wealth over the three-year period. Although the nominal total value of the investment, with the interest compounded, increased to $13,310, the value in real dollars, after taxes, reflects a zero-percent rate of return. Many investors deceive themselves by failing to do this kind of investment analysis.

When you place your funds in a certificate of deposit, you transfer to the bank the opportunity to earn the higher yields that your money could have earned for you. Your losses become even larger if you need for any reason to withdraw your funds prior to maturity. If you do, the bank will impose horrendous penalties for early withdrawal. CDs are liquid in the sense of access to your funds, but the price of that access is outrageously severe.

Unless your crystal ball tells you that interest rates are going to plunge over the near term, avoid bank CDs or keep your maturities short. If you choose a CD for some of your funds, don't hesitate to shop around for the most favorable rates. They vary substantially, depending on the hunger of the lending institution for additional deposits.

Money-market Funds

Money-market funds (other mutual funds are discussed in Chapter 5) are a form of cash equivalents, with the same drawbacks and advantages. Generally speaking, they pay higher yields than the various bank instruments discussed above. Money-market funds are an appropriate parking place for emergency money or money for which you have a foreseeable need in the relatively near future.

Once you have accumulated enough money to pay three months of expenses, a money-market fund also becomes a cop out. Their earnings are inadequate, they have no tax advantages, and they are subject to inflation.

Your best bet in investing in any of these is to consider a family of funds with a good track record that will give you the flexibility to move your money quickly if better investment opportunities appear.

Short-term Government Securities

These are primarily Treasury bills and Treasury notes. All are backed by the full faith and credit of the U.S. Government, so they are considered totally free of any risk of default. Not only are they a conservative investment, they are also very short-term. T-bills are auctioned weekly in 3-month and 6-month versions, and issued monthly in one-year maturities. Because they are short-term, they show less volatility in the value of their principal than is the case with longer-term debt instruments. The minimum denomination is $10,000, which precludes their purchase by many small investors.

T-notes are medium-term instruments, going out up to 7 years (bonds go out beyond 7 years). Both forms of security are subject to federal income tax, but not to state and local taxes. If you buy them directly from a Federal Reserve bank, rather than through a broker or commercial banker, you can eliminate fees that would otherwise reduce your yield.

These federal securities are usually purchased by people with the "Depression syndrome," who still behave as though they were living in deflationary times. Many of these people are negative in their outlook about the economy. They have little confidence in their own ability to manage money and are too suspicious to allow a professional to manage it for them, or to entrust it to a financial institution. They sacrifice the potential of higher yields to obtain security, peace of mind, and the avoidance of making financial decisions.

This is not to imply that Treasury securities are not a legitimate investment. In some situations they are. But the decision to buy them should be a rational choice, not one based on emotional, psychological considerations. Never forget that no one investment is the correct one at all times for all of one's assets. Your portfolio should be under constant surveillance, and altered as your needs and market conditions dictate.

Financial Supermarkets

These are corporations whose primary business in the past has been something other than financial services: Prudential, an insurance company; Sears, a mass merchandiser; Merrill Lynch, a securities broker. Their emergence as major financial conglomerates has been made possible by the same deregulation process that has produced such chaos— and so many new opportunities—for traditional banking firms.

If you can afford the minimum deposit required for their asset-management accounts, usually $15,000 or $20,000, these organizations and others may be worth exploring. They offer accounts accessible by toll-free telephones or automatic-teller machines that you can use for checking, credit card payments, and consumer loans. The automatic sweep feature assures that any surplus in your account is automatically invested at prevailing money-market rates. To entice you further, there are various bells and whistles ranging from free travelers' checks to discount brokerage services to personal financial planning assistance.

On the whole, this intense competition is likely to be good for small investors. But it means, once again, that it is increasingly important to *pay attention*! The rapid-fire changes in the financial markets are confusing for consumers, who may be tempted to sit things out until the dust settles. As in most other things, procrastination is rarely a virtue. Keep well informed, read the analyses as well as the advertising, and be ready to take advantage of the best of the new financial instruments that are suited to your needs.

Conventional Life Insurance

It may seem inappropriate to include this topic here, since insurance is covered in a separate chapter. It belongs here because the purchase of conventional whole-life insurance is one of those knee-jerk decisions that people still make: a noninvestment investment.

Whole-life insurance combines insurance protection with a nominal savings function. You pay level premiums over the years, during which your actuarial risk of death rises significantly. During the early years, the insurance company invests the difference—for a far greater return to them than the cash value the company will pay you. This is analogous to what happens to your accounts at savings institutions.

If you already own whole-life and have been paying the premiums for a number of years, it is an excellent source of low-cost capital. By all means use it. You can borrow against your policy's value at below-market rates. Alternatively, explore the possibility of converting the cash value of your policy into a universal life plan (see Chapter 9). It's more efficient, and you can do a tax-free exchange from one policy to the other.

But if you have no conventional life insurance, don't buy any. If you are relatively young and need only insurance protection, buy term insurance. It is much cheaper, because all you pay for is what you need: the protection. If you want insurance plus a high-yield savings plan, consider universal life.

Gambling: The Other End of the Spectrum

Most of the noninvestment investments described so far are losers because inflation erodes the value of your money or because the financial institution makes most of the profit, or both. Sometimes they are not as safe as they appear.

No one thinks of Atlantic City or Las Vegas as safe. Yet some people "invest" in markets that are akin to that of gambling. Most option trading falls into that category (see Chapter 6).

One of the worst offenders is commodity-futures trading. This is high-stakes gambling, make no mistake. You can hear amazing stories of the amount of money someone made by cornering the market in spring wheat or pork bellies. The stories may even be true, but don't be dazzled. Between 85 and 90 percent of commodity speculators lose money, and that tells the story. We do not put our clients' money in commodities—ever. If you don't want to be a loser, don't speculate in commodities.

In summary, consider the increasing number of cash-equivalent instruments as a good place for money you need to keep in a holding pattern. But do not fool yourself that this constitutes any sort of investment plan. Once you move beyond the minimal amounts of savings required for an emergency fund, you should become conversant with a far broader range of investments. This knowledge will enable you to plan a suitably diversified portfolio and increase your household resources.

CHAPTER 4

COMMON STOCKS

Today, those looking for high yields don't have to risk their assets in the stock market. Stocks are no longer the only game in town. There are many other investments with net returns of 12, 15, or even 20 percent that involve only nominal risk. I advise most of my clients to avoid common stocks, unless they protect themselves with stop-loss orders or put options. Given the risk of loss of capital, I classify common stocks as an investment loser. The object is to invest your funds comfortably as well as profitably, and most investors are not comfortable with a product as volatile and speculative as common stocks.

Although they are temperamentally, psychologically, and emotionally unsuited to investing in "the market," many new clients are fanatically devoted to stocks that they already hold and to stocks as an investment category. One of our clients is a widow with a handicapped adult son who will need lifelong care. Her late husband worked for a major manufacturer with an employee stock-option plan, and she accumulated shares now worth approximately $250,000. When he died, his pension benefits stopped, leaving the widow with an investment that currently yields about 1 percent in dividends. She has some other income, but we could make her life and her son's much more comfortable by selling the stock and switching her to an investment with a higher yield. She is adamant in her refusal because her husband once told her never to sell, and it makes her feel guilty if she even thinks about selling. As a result, she and her son are suffering unnecessarily.

When you have your financial foundation in place and have a base of serious money that will enable you to achieve your planned goals, *only then* should you consider participating in the stock market. Common stocks are truly suitable only for those willing to take a risk with aggressive fun money. For that risk to pay off, everything must be right, especially the timing of your entry into and withdrawal from the market.

Even if you can afford to lose some of your assets and won't lose any sleep if you do, you can't afford to be careless. *If* you buy at the right time, *if* the industry is right, *if* the stock is right, *if* its earnings are continuing to grow, *if* its management is competent, *if* the economy is strong, and *if* you know when to sell, you might make money or even get rich. That's a lot of ifs. The main point to remember, if you do decide to take a flyer in the stock market, is this: Don't be too proud or too greedy to cut your losses short and let your profits ride.

Within the stock market your risk tolerance should dictate your portfolio. The most defensive plays are high-yielding stocks in very stable industries like food or utilities. Conservative investors favor income stocks, those of companies with long histories of dividend payments. The more aggressive invest in emerging growth stocks (for example, computer software companies or biogenetic firms), cyclical or interest-rate-sensitive industries, or companies that are targets for mergers or leveraged buyouts.

Every stock investor, and the aggressive one in particular, needs someone knowledgeable and trustworthy who will do the homework necessary to select the investments that are appropriate and suitable. For example, we put our aggressive clients into Walt Disney Productions when it was a takeover target in 1984, priced at $49 a share. Six months later, just before the company bought its way out of the takeover threat, we sold them out for $70. Once the takeover attempt ended, the stock went right back to $49. Subsequently, after a major management change, the stock again began to appreciate.

However, the fact that we suggest taking advantage of investment advice does not imply that you are absolved from studying the market yourself and monitoring the performance of the stocks that you hold. This chapter will help you to do that by describing what the stock market is and how it works, suggesting some stock market strategies, and revealing some techniques for minimizing your risk in stock market investing.

What Common Stocks Are

Shares of common stock represent an equity or ownership interest in a corporation. A corporation exists ''by grace of the state'' where it is chartered, which sets the maximum amount of stock the company can issue. The monetary total of common and preferred stock, and bonds issued, is the company's capitalization. Money paid in for common stock becomes the permanent capital of the firm. The number of shares you own in relation to the total number outstanding establishes your proportional equity in the corporation's assets, your proportional earnings, and your voting power. Dividends represent that portion of earnings that is paid out in cash or additional stock. Most corporations retain some portion of earnings each year to permit expansion and growth.

One basic right of shareholders is to transfer ownership of their stock. They may also have rights or privileges to buy additional securities at a specified price.

Because they have relatively low unit cost and no fixed

term, stocks can be used in an investment portfolio to meet a variety of objectives and to implement strategies ranging from long-term reliable income to short-term trading and rampant speculation. Stockholders can benefit from a profitable company through dividends and capital appreciation (a rise in the value of their shares).

Warrants

Some stocks come with warrants. Warrants are privileges to buy additional stock under specified conditions, usually at a price higher than the market at the time the warrant is issued. Subsequently, if the value of the stock increases, you profit from buying the stock at a below-market price. Warrants may or may not be detachable from the security with which they are issued. Since warrants represent a call on the future earnings of a corporation, their value is speculative and their price fluctuates widely. In these respects they are similar to options, and I do not recommend trading in them.

Preferred Stocks

Preferred stocks are a combination of debt and equity with a fixed dividend regardless of the company's market performance. They have a priority over common stock in the payment of dividends, usually in the distribution of assets, and they confer no voting rights. Because of this priority, many believe that they are safer than common stocks. They may, if the corporation encounters financial disaster, offer an additional margin of protection against loss of capital, but to get it you pay a substantial price. Individuals should never buy preferred stock for income. In my opinion, only corporations, who get an 85-percent tax exemption on the dividends, should own preferred shares.

How Stocks Are Traded: Brokers and Dealers

Brokers buy and sell for the account and risk of others. They make their money from fees or commissions on the sale of securities or other financial products. If you trade through a broker, you should be aware that the Securities Investor Protection Corporation (SIPC) provides insurance to protect investors against brokerage firm failures. Over 8,100 brokerage firms are SIPC members.

A dealer buys for his own account and risk. He makes a market when he quotes prices at which he is willing to buy or sell a security; the combined bid and offering price quotation is his market. Most dealers are specialized in particular securities. Dealers who have an inventory of a security for trading purposes are said to have a "position" in the security. They obtain their profits through the *spread* between bids and offers, which must produce enough revenue to compensate for the risk in taking a position, plus their business expenses. The spread is narrowest for U.S. Government bonds and widest for inactive securities; i.e., it tends to increase in accordance with the efforts and risks involved in finding buyers and sellers.

How Stocks Are Traded: Exchanges and the OTC Market

The primary functions of the organized exchanges are to provide a meeting place for buyers and sellers of listed securities and to report on their transactions. The exchanges provide marketability for securities and publicity for the financial activities of listed companies—both very helpful functions for investors.

Organized exchanges like the New York Stock Exchange (NYSE, about 1,600 companies) and the American Stock Exchange (AMEX, about 850 companies) are regulated by the Securities and Exchange Commission (SEC). Trading is done through brokers or commission houses who are members of the exchange and act for the buyers and sellers. The system is like a two-sided auction market, with the priority to the first bid or offer at an agreed price, and no secret transactions permitted.

The other broad marketplace where trading occurs in even larger dollar volumes than on organized exchanges is the over-the-counter market. It provides facilities for the initial distribution of numerous new issues and for trading in smaller, less-established companies, as well as government obligations and a number of listed securities (especially when large blocks must be sold quickly).

The over-the-counter market has no fixed location or exchange floor; rather, it is now operated by the National Association of Securities Dealers through its Automated Quotations System (NASDAQ). Generally, the OTC market is where the securities of small young companies are first publicly offered to investors. It currently has almost four thousand companies, many more than the largest formal exchanges, including many of the most interesting, young, high-growth companies.

The basic information for the NASDAQ system is provided by dealer firms that have been qualified by NASD as "market makers." Using electronic terminals, they update their bid/asked quotes throughout the business day. Unlike the single "specialist," the dealer who serves as the market maker for any given NYSE-listed stock, companies that trade over-the-counter usually have several market makers, which increases competition in stock pricing and offers at least good liquidity to investors.

NASDAQ also computes a negotiated quotation based on median bid and spread. Thus, the OTC market is a negotiation market, unlike the stock-exchange auction markets. Newspaper quotations and the National Quotation Bureau reporting service make OTC market information widely available.

Penny Stocks

So-called "penny stocks" are low-priced offerings (generally $5 a share or less) that are traded over-the-counter or on the smaller exchanges, such as the Denver Stock Exchange. These are highly speculative investments, often in fledgling companies launched by ambitious entrepreneurs. They are often first offered by an underwriter, usually an investment banker, who often syndicates the initial sale and agrees either to market the issue or to guarantee purchase of the shares for resale. (Subsequently, the stock may be available through NASDAQ as a secondary market.)

When you buy a new issue, you pay no commission. This may appear to be a bargain unless you are aware that a year after the initial offering only a third of new issues are likely to be trading above their offering price, and that some of the companies may already be down the tube. As with any other investment, the key to investing in new issues is to make sure you are getting value for your money rather than relying on a "hot tip" and later finding, to your sorrow, that you simply financed the failed dream of a starry-eyed entrepreneur.

The early 1980s were a hot time for initial public offerings; many investors jumped in, believing there was a chance to make quick profits. Some did, but during the same period, fraud accusations and other scandals sent the penny market reeling. It has since recovered. Newsletters such as *Going Public* and *Penny Stock Journal* offer detailed current information. I do not recommend penny stocks for my clients or for you, unless you are seeking an alternative to Las Vegas. They are gambles, not investments.

While the Denver Stock Exchange specializes in new issues, some local stock exchanges specialize in public companies that have filed for bankruptcy and have been delisted from the New York or American Stock Exchanges. Some of these highflier stocks that have fallen on hard times subsequently recover rather well, as did Braniff International Airlines. These stocks, like new issues, offer the aggressive investor a chance to get in at low prices.

General Influences on Stock Prices

The stock market, representing as it does the shares of thousands of publicly held corporations, is intrinsically volatile. This is increasingly so because of the growing presence of large institutional investors in the market—banks, pension funds, insurance companies, and mutual funds. As these investors move in and out of the market, purchasing or selling large blocks of stock and often following each other like sheep, they can cause major sudden swings in stock prices.

Many variables influence the decisions of the managers of institutional portfolios, some of which are equally important to the individual investor. The business cycle of expansion, inflation, recession, and recovery is one such factor. The Federal Reserve's monetary policy is another. When the Fed tightens the money supply, often in response to an increase in the inflation rate, interest rates tend to rise. This in turn has negative effects on all stock prices, because money tends to flow out into liquid cash equivalents when their yields rise. In addition, some industries are highly interest-sensitive. Housing construction is an example.

Economic forecasts; the release of statistics on productivity, imports, or the gross national product (GNP); foreign events; and anticipated changes in fiscal policy and the tax laws by the administration or Congress will all affect stock prices. If you keep up with current events, you will be aware of changes in the economic climate that may affect your investments.

The direction of corporate earnings is another indicator of which way stock prices are heading. When profits and earnings are strong, stocks are usually better values. Declining earnings will usually be followed by a decline in stock prices. The analysts never seem to be at a loss to provide a specific reason for daily shifts in the direction of the market, but, in truth, this movement is often purely psychological.

How Stock Are Traded: The Mechanics

Most stock purchases are made with *market orders*, which simply instruct the broker to buy (or sell) at the market price. No specific price is called for; the broker is required to execute the order at the best price obtainable in the market at that time. A second kind of instruction is the limit order, which does specify a price. If your order says to buy at $50.00, the order cannot be executed at a price higher than $50.00; if your order is to sell at $50.00, it cannot be executed at any price lower than that. A *day order* expires at the close of business on the day it is placed, a *week* or *month order* at the close of the last business day of the period in question. *Good 'til cancel* (GTC) orders remain open indefinitely, until the requested shares are purchased. *Limit orders* specify a price at which the transaction is to take place.

Stock are usually sold in *round lots*, the number of shares in a trading unit on the exchanges (normally 100). *Odd lots* are anything less. Odd-lot dealers usually execute orders $1/8$ point away from the price of the next round-lot sale, taking the difference as their commission. This commission is in addition to the one you pay your broker for executing the trade, so it is preferable to buy in round lots if possible.

Margin Accounts

Most clients' accounts with their brokers are cash accounts, and that is how their stock transactions are handled. If your order is executed today, you will be expected to have the cash in the hands of your broker to pay for it five business days later, on *settlement day*. For greater leverage and flexibility, but also with greater risk of loss, you can open a margin account. Essentially, this is a means of buying on credit, borrowing up to half the cost of your stock purchases from your broker. The amount you may borrow varies with the type of security and with federal margin requirements, as well as with the brokerage firm's policies. The broker charges you interest on the loan, in addition to his commission and any taxes due. Because of these costs, it is difficult to make profits on a small margin account. Such accounts are really a tool for the larger investor.

Margin-maintenance requirements are intended to keep your account's debits from getting out of hand in the event the prices of your stocks decline. A margin-maintenance call means you must put up more cash or deliver more marketable securities as collateral, or you must sell some of your holdings to reduce the debit. If your account becomes "undermargined" (falls below minimum requirements), your broker can liquidate your securities. If you guess right about a stock you bought on margin, your gains are larger. If you guess wrong, you lose bigger. Margin trading is subject to the general rule: Don't borrow to speculate.

Selling Short

It is axiomatic that most investors buy stock in the hope that its value will increase. Investors who sell short believe that the stock price will decline, and they gamble that they are right by selling stock that they do not own. They do this by borrowing the stock from their broker through their margin account and selling it at the current market price for delivery at a specified future date.

For example, let's assume that ABC Company's stock is at $30 a share. You believe it is overvalued and will drop to $22 within a month. You order your broker to sell 100 shares of ABC short. If the stock does indeed drop to $22 before the date on which the transaction is closed, you cover your position by delivering an equal quantity of stock (bought at $22) and make a profit of $800 on the difference (minus commissions, of course).

However (and here is the risk), if you have miscalculated and ABC stock rises to $40 during the interim before the contracted delivery date, you still must deliver the stock, and you will lose the difference between the market price when the transaction was initiated and the current higher price. In this case, that's $10 a share for 100 shares. You're out $1,000.

Selling short is equivalent to rolling dice. For the possibility of limited profit, you subject yourself to the potential of unlimited losses. And even if you win, your profits will be taxed as ordinary income, not a long-term capital gain.

If you bought this book because you are risk-averse, stay away from short sales!

Choosing Individual Stocks

Careful research is in order before you select the stocks in which you wish to invest. I use the approach called *fundamental analysis,* which I have found most useful among the many techniques that professional analysts use. The first step is to analyze general economic trends to determine whether this is a good time to enter the market. Next, examine the potential of the industry to which the company you have chosen belongs. Then focus on the specifics of that company: earnings, dividends, financial statement, and analysis. What is the company's competitive position within its industry, and what is the trend? Is it improving, stable, or has its position declined? How strong is its management? Is the company working hard to find new profit opportunities and expand its markets?

When I have answered these qualitative questions to my satisfaction, I turn to four basic calculations that indicate the worth of a particular stock: earnings per share, price–earnings ratio, yield, and net asset value per share.

Earnings per share are computed by taking net corporate earnings after taxes, subtracting preferred dividends, and dividing the remainder by the number of shares outstanding. Both present and future dividends depend on earnings, and a stock's market price will tend to reflect the growth or decline of its earnings per share.

The *price–earnings ratio* is the market price of the stock divided by the current per-share earnings of the corporation. It is a conventional and highly regarded indicator of value because it measures prices against earning power. A high P/E ratio is justified only if a company's earnings are expected to increase. A historical review of a stock's P/E ratios is instructive in estimating current value relative to the past.

Yield is the annual cash dividend as a proportion of the current market price, and it is expressed as a percentage. It is also an indicator of the reasonableness of the stock's market price. Studying dividend yield history can provide another basis for stock valuation.

The *net asset value*, or book value per share, attempts to measure the assets a corporation has working for each share of common stock. To compute it, take the net balance sheet value of the corporate assets, subtract the total of creditors' and preferred stockholders' claims, and divide the remainder by the number of common shares. Theoretically, this number, compared with the current market price of the company's stock, should tell you whether you would get more or less than the market price of your stock if the company were liquidated. However, book value is based on cost, not earning power, and does not factor in intangible assets, which may be substantial. Thus, asset value is not a totally reliable measure.

Another basis for estimating stock value is to measure its performance in relation to major market barometers such as the Standard & Poor's 500-Stock Index or the *New York Times* Index, or perhaps to one of the narrower Dow Jones indices.

Yet another indicator is *beta,* an index of stock volatility. A stock that rises and falls with the market will have a beta of 1, whereas a stock that moves up and down in wider swings may have a beta of 1.5 and be highly volatile, with precipitous drops during bear markets. Go for betas of one or less unless you have nerves of steel. The Value Line Investment Survey publishes beta figures.

Your broker, major business publications, and investment advisory newsletters are other sources of information on a company's financial performance, management quality, and prospects. Standard & Poor's and Moody's publish major financial reference works, including historic information. For the greatest detail, write the company that interests you for its latest annual report. Read the financial statements and trend data carefully before you invest.

Stock Investment Strategies

One mistake frequently made by beginning investors, and even by seasoned ones who should know better, is inconsistency: buying and selling particular issues on tips or whims and without an overall strategy. Since the market will always have more losers, a random approach is unlikely to

serve you well over the long term, even though you may
luck into an occasional "killing."

Wealth comes to those who develop and act on a consistent strategy that fits their investment objectives. One sen-
sible approach in stock selection is to study the quality of
the company's management. Read everything you can find
that evaluates management performance and behavior. Determine whether the executives earn a substantial portion
of their compensation from stock options or legitimate bonuses for corporate results, rather than from salary alone.
The term "incentive bonus" means exactly what it says: the
corporate directors have adopted a plan to give management an incentive to improve the company's results. If the
company's performance improves, they profit, and as a
shareholder, so do you.

Your basic investment strategy will be determined by your
objectives. There are three major categories and, for some
investors, combinations of the three:

Investing for income
This is a conservative strategy appropriate for older
investors and the most risk-averse. Look for consistent dividend growth over several years, low betas, and a debt-to-
equity ratio of 67 percent or less. Certain utilities may be a
good base for such a strategy, as may the stocks of out-of-
favor industries that are currently in a low-priced phase,
but that may be expected to rise in price during the next
phase of the business cycle.

Investing for growth
An aggressive strategy best suited to younger investors
with plenty of time to wait for a small company to hit the
big time—or to recover from their losses if they make a
mistake. These companies' prices are apt to be volatile, and
they have no established track record. Look for an annual

average earnings growth of 20 percent or more for the past five years, a P/E of less than 20, and 15 to 25 percent on equity (which shows how effectively management uses the shareholders' funds). Also be certain that the company is not burdened with too much debt; long-term debt should not exceed the value of outstanding common stock. Some experts suggest this rule of thumb for purchasing such stocks: If the P/E ratio is half the five-year average growth rate, the stock is a bargain.

Investing for total return on undervalued assets

The cautiously aggressive investor is most likely to opt for this strategy. Many once solid companies, and even some solid ones, fall on hard times in the stock market—often for reasons that have little or nothing to do with their future potential. Often these setbacks are aberrations related to the business cycle, with the company bouncing back as that cycle moves into the next phase. For example, the machine-tool industry suffers during periods of tight money and high inflation when its industrial customers shun major capital investments; but the industry, or at least its leaders, tend to recover nicely during the maturing stages of an economic expansion.

Stock prices of strong companies may also decline when large institutional investors desert them to dash off in pursuit of an alternative that suddenly seems more attractive. When several of them dump large blocks of stock, the price declines.

During depressed periods, when a company's earnings and share prices are down, its net assets may actually be worth far more than its total shareholders equity. When the stock's price is less than half its book value per share, the company may be a real bargain. Even in the worst case, if it goes into bankruptcy, its assets (buildings, natural resources, land, machinery) could be liquidated to pay off creditors and shareholders. And those same assets make such a company attractive to takeover specialists, or to other companies seeking to diversify. Look for P/E multiples under 10 and stock prices less than 75 percent of book value. Also note such macroeconomic factors as whether the government would let the sick company die. (Remember Lockheed? Chrysler?) In a strategic industry like steel or oil or defense manufacturing, Uncle Sam may step in to prevent the company from folding.

This type of strategy, if it matches your objectives and if you time your buy/sell decisions well, can be profitable over the long term. However, you must be consistent, attentive, and patient.

Investment Techniques

Your broker calls with a stock recommendation and you buy XYZ Company at $25 a share. Six months later the stock is at $15 and he calls again to urge you to buy more. This is a strategy known as *dollar cost averaging*. The theory is that if you bought shares at $25 and later buy an equal number at $15, you will have recovered your loss if the stock rises $5 rather than $10. I consider this to be imprudent strategy. You don't buy a stock to bring your cost basis down; you buy to make money. Buying more of a loser is like borrowing money to stay at the craps table because you are going to recover your losses on the next roll of the dice. If you bought a loser, accept your ill fortune and get out.

Better still, don't put yourself in a position to sustain a major loss. If you had hedged your stock purchases correctly in the first place, as described later in this chapter, you would have been out at $22. Dollar cost averaging is a loser. Cut your losses, and let your profits run. That's smart investing.

Many investors employ *systematic purchase plans* to force themselves to invest a fixed portion of their income on a regular basis. On average, you will pay slightly below market for stock purchased this way, but you may be charged higher commissions because you are buying odd lots. Unless you must have the discipline of forced saving, this approach is not ideal. You will probably do better if you retain the flexibility to select your stocks on the basis of current information and buy it in round lots. Some small investors increase their holdings gradually through *dividend reinvestment plans*. Because their dividend checks are small, they might reinvest them by participating in a reinvestment plan that is done for them.

Market Timing

Timing is the most important factor in buying stocks, probably more so than in making other types of investments. But to get it right, you have to pay attention. The market anticipates good news and discounts bad news up to six months in advance, so clever timing should be more than up-to-date—it should be prescient. Your investment philosophy and instincts and even your intuition about factors that will affect the overall economy can govern your timing of buy-and-sell decisions.

For example, if the market, on balance, is rising, if the industry you're considering is a market leader now, if your stock's earnings are rising each year, and the company's management is strong—buy now. This is buying bullishly, on the anticipation of good news.

On the other hand, you can also buy on bad news, which is somewhat more risky. This is *contrarian* investing, buying when most investors are bearish, and it sometimes pays off handsomely. But be warned: it is not for the impatient or the faint of heart! Contrarians look first at a stock's historic trading range and consider buying when it is near its three-to-five-year low. Then they examine its five-year earnings history and current projections. If earnings are at the low end of that range but estimates of future earnings are positive, that may point to a turnaround in the price of the stock. If the stock is selling at less than its book value, that's another positive factor.

Another clue to watch in stock market investing: *insider trading.* If you follow the smart money, you may profit as well. Corporate officers and directors seem to possess an uncanny knack for buying their own companies' shares low and selling them high. That's not surprising, of course, because however diligently you study a company, you can't possibly know as much about its prospects as the people who work there. If one corporate insider sells a block of stock, that may simply mean that he had need for the money. But if several officers suddenly begin unloading—or buying—it may have real significance. Several services keep track of insider buys and sells; ask your investment adviser to keep you abreast of these trends both for stock you own (or plan to buy) and for the market as a whole.

Here are some *don't*s with respect to timing:

Don't buy common stocks with money you think you'll need in less than one year. You don't want to be forced to sell when the time isn't opportune.

Don't move a substantial portion of your wealth into or out of the market at one time.

Don't follow *anyone's* "infallible" system. The only infallible systems I've ever seen were those that, sooner or later, couldn't fail to lose. Use your own common sense and good judgment. Don't let yourself be stampeded.

Industry Groups

In researching stocks for investment, strive for reasonable diversification among industries. Each industry has its ups and downs, but, except during a general recession, they don't move together. When you examine a company, ask yourself or your investment adviser whether the industry it is in provides widely used and needed products or services for which demand is substantial and growing. Is the industry cyclical or relatively stable? Is it likely to be adversely affected by international developments? For example, does its raw materials come primarily from politically unstable parts of the world, so it would be threatened by a political upheaval there? Note the industry's labor situation. Are its leading companies about to renegotiate major labor contracts? Have there been strike threats? What is the trend in the use of its products or services? Is it dependent largely on a few products that may be obsolescent because of emerging technology, or is it diversified?

Another element to consider is whether an industry is generating takeover interest. Mergers and acquisitions tend to sweep through entire industries. In 1983–84 it was energy companies, in 1985 the broadcast and communications industry. Follow these trends with care; they may afford the potential for big gains if your timing is on target. But, as always, don't buy solely on the possibility of a quick profit. Buy on corporate fundamentals and market value, and if a takeover is in prospect, that's frosting on the cake.

Let's look at the pros and cons of investing in three different industries today: utilities, airlines, and homebuilding.

Utilities

Utility stocks are a favorite of many conservative investors, particularly those who are seeking consistent income. I know families that have held the same utility stock for generations. However, if they are attractive to you, be aware that all utilities are not the same in terms of quality, risk, or growth potential. These differences, which have been magnified by the move into atomic energy, mean that more homework is required. Very high yields don't mean that the company is safe and, indeed, in some instances could be a warning that a serious adjustment may be forthcoming, and the company may reduce or eliminate its dividend.

Within the utilities industry, there are at least four groups:

1. Companies that have moved vigorously into nuclear development. Favorites a few years ago, many of these companies are in serious trouble. They can't get their plants on line, they have huge cost overruns, and their stock has dropped substantially. One example—there are many others—is Public Service of Indiana. When it canceled its Marble Hill nuclear plant in 1983, after cost estimates rose from $5 billion to $7 billion, its price dropped from $26 to $19 almost overnight. Subsequently, its value has continued to drop.

Some investors have made speculative investments in problem utilities after they crashed, hoping for a strong comeback. I don't recommend it, because it is a dangerous game.

2. Utilities involved in nuclear development that have not yet demonstrated outward signs of trouble. Their nuclear facilities are not yet on line. If cost overruns appear, or they experience difficulty in getting government certification, they may join the firms in category 1.

3. Total-return utilities. These firms are not heavily nuclear, and the plants they have are operating successfully within government guidelines. They were built without massive cost overruns. Most of the companies in this category have been extremely successful over the past ten or fifteen years, showing high profitability. These companies suffered only slight discounting from their highs during the mid-1980s selloff and are relatively good investments now.

4. Firms with no nuclear plants. People who want safety, high yield, and no nuclear risk have a very positive reaction to these stocks. They include the top six or eight utilities in

the country. When the emotional selloff is over, such companies will be very good candidates indeed, because they're underpriced.

Under the best circumstances, utilities still offer relative safety, high yield, tax benefits, and good long-term potential for appreciation. Thus, utilities can be a good low-risk investment if you do your homework and choose wisely.

Airlines

In the early stages of deregulation, with fuel costs also soaring, the airlines took a beating. There were more carriers on more routes with more available seats than the traffic would bear, and competitive pressures brought indiscriminate discounting and heavy losses. There is still price competition, but today it is structured for the most part so that the full-fare passengers are still locked in, and otherwise empty seats filled by new reduced-fare passengers. Revenue passenger load factors, the measure of airline profitability, are soaring. Meanwhile, the costs of borrowing, fuel, and labor have declined, and foreign travel is sometimes encouraged by the strong dollar in overseas markets.

As a result of these positive factors, airline profits are up, and airline executives are smiling again. Investors who select and buy airlines with the greatest potential for increased earnings will probably be smiling, too. At the moment, several airlines are also being eyed as takeover candidates, which also tends to drive their prices up.

Homebuilding

Residential construction is a feast-or-famine industry, extremely sensitive to mortgage interest rates. Housing is unique in that consumer demand consistently exceeds supply. The prosperity of the industry depends on the ability of eager customers to qualify for mortgage loans so that they can buy.

When interest rates are declining, home ownership be-comes a reality for increasing numbers of families, and the industry thrives. When they are rising, many potential buy-ers are excluded from the market because they lack suffi-cient income to manage the debt-service costs. Housing quickly starts to decline. Thus, investors in this industry must be extremely watchful regarding the prospective course of mortgage interest rates because the value of shares in homebuilding firms will be grossly affected by changes in either direction. A more detailed discussion of real estate investments will be found in Chapter 13.

Hedging Against Stock Market Risk

I have already warned that the stock market is not the place for most investors to be with most of their money, but this does not imply that all risk-averse investors must or should avoid stocks altogether. There are ways to mini-mize stock market risk, and in the remainder of this chapter I will discuss them.

Diversification

Diversifying your portfolio among different types of in-vestments is a sound principle for minimizing risk, but di-viding your stock holdings among too many companies may dilute the positive effects of diversification. Buy shares in industries that meet your investment objectives, but not in more companies than you and your adviser can monitor adequately. A maximum of eight or ten stocks should pro-vide the diversification you want without taxing your abil-ity to keep track of their performance.

Diversification minimizes risk of the probability that losses in one stock will be offset by gains in another. However, it does not protect against a broad decline in the overall market, so it is far from foolproof for those who will tolerate no more than minimum risk.

This is also true of another technique used by investment analysts, known as *charting*. This involves examination of past market cycles and performance trends in an attempt to forecast what may happen to stock prices in the future. Technical analysis also attempts to fathom investor psychology and predict broad changes stemming from their behavior. The technique can be a useful way to predict major turnarounds in the marketplace or major moves in particular industries—whether they are at the top or the bottom of a cycle.

The indicators that technical analysts watch are called the resistance and support levels. The *resistance level* is the price at which selling is expected to overcome demand and temporarily halt or reverse a price advance; the *support level* is the price at which buying is expected to become active enough to stop or reverse a decline. I use such indicators, but I'm basically a fundamentalist. I look at the earnings, the management, the industry, and *then* I look at the chart. I count what I see there for only about 10 percent of my decision. All the other elements must be right; charting is a technique I use only for confirmation of a decision based on other factors.

There are a number of ways to protect yourself against substantial loss of capital because of a decline in the value of the stocks you hold. One of the most common is the *stop-loss order*, which enables you to determine your approximate degree of loss potential. You do this by giving your broker an order to sell a stock if it sustains a specific drop in price. If your stock is at 40, you can order it sold if it drops to 37, limiting your maximum loss to about 9 percent. You can keep revising the amount of the order upward to protect your gain if the stock price rises. Thus, you let your profits ride, but cut your losses short.

Two forms of options can be used to hedge stock purchases. One is selling calls on stock you already own, which is known as *writing covered calls.* When you sell a call you give the buyer the right to buy your stock at a specified price at a future date. For this you receive a premium, which affords some downside protection against loss. But in exchange for that extra income, you limit your upside potential without substantial protection on the downside.

Buying put options

You can "insure" the assets you invest in stocks by purchasing put options on the stocks at the same time you make your initial purchases. Put options are contracts that give you the right to sell the stock for a specified price (the "strike price") within a specified time period. You pay a premium for this insurance, which ensures that your stock holding will not fall below the strike price. If the stock declines during that time, your put acts as an insurance contract which limits your loss.

The difference between these forms of insurance is control. If you put in a stop-loss order or even a covered call, you lose control. On the other hand, when you buy a put, while you incur the cost of that put, you retain control for however long that put goes out in time. These options are discussed more fully in Chapter 6.

Stock index futures

If you are a large investor, you might consider hedging your stock portfolio by purchasing a relatively new instrument—stock index futures. These assign a cash value to each point of change in an index—for example, the Standard & Poor's 500 Index. As a market-weighted broadly based index, it is a good proxy for the market. The futures contracts are traded on the Chicago Mercantile Exchange.

Trading in index futures hedges against risks that broadly affect the market, known as market or systematic risks. To determine the correct number of futures contracts to sell to make a reasonable balance between the contracts and his portfolio, the investor must examine the beta average of his stock portfolio. Losses in your stock portfolio are offset by gains in the futures, and vice versa. One advantage is that this can be accomplished without the transaction costs inherent in selling some stocks and purchasing others (or other products).

International Investing and ADRs

Trading in foreign companies can be accomplished in several ways. Some companies are traded over-the-counter in the United States. Some are available to American investors only by using American Depository Receipts (ADRs), essentially a matter of buying the stocks through a financial institution. Usually stock purchased this way does not carry voting rights. Several mutual-fund sponsors operate mutual funds that are partly or solely invested in overseas securities; some of these professionally managed funds have excellent performance records.

Last, you may consider direct investment in foreign stocks through international exchanges, such as those in Hong Kong or London. The pace of trading is fast and furious. Unlike the formal stock exchanges in the United States, foreign ones are unregulated, and things can get pretty wild. Most American investors are not sufficiently well versed in the operation of these markets to invest directly. If you want a piece of the action in foreign securities, choose one of the other alternatives.

Knowing When to Sell

People often complain to me, "My stockbroker always calls to tell me when it's time to buy, but never when to sell." Remember, it's your money, not your stockbroker's.

You do need to know when to sell, but preferably, you should make this decision when you originally invest. For example, if you purchase the stock of an asset-rich company that is currently selling for 50 percent of its book value per share, you may decide to sell when the price reaches 100 percent of book value. If its performance is below expectations, if the stock shows little or no change in six months or a year, you may wish to sell. (Of course, you have protected yourself against a major decline with a stop-loss order or a put hedge.)

Remember, the overall purpose of investing is to earn the best possible return on your capital. The best strategy is to sell when the stock rises to more than it is worth relative to other investments. When your money can earn a higher return elsewhere, it is time to move. The rule of thumb here is: When the price of a security you own is so high you would not consider it a good buy today, consider selling it. Concentrate on value rather than movement.

And don't cry if the stock goes up after you sell, as long as you got out with a profit. Don't let greed get the best of you. The stock market is a percentage game, not an ego game. Limit your risks, follow your strategy faithfully, and you'll be in a better position to profit in the stock market than 90 percent of the other investors. Ideally, in your portfolio, you should have six or seven different stocks. Not all of them will go down at the same time; some will ride the other way. You really need a financial adviser to help you with the selection. The point is that as a cautious investor, *you can be in the stock market with only nominal risk.* If the bottom falls out of the market, and you have placed a stop-loss order, your maximum risk will be 8 to 10 percent in the worst case. That is the only safe way to use the market to your advantage, to sustain or improve the value of your holdings with only nominal risk. Using these techniques, you can put predictability into an unpredictable market.

CHAPTER 5

MUTUAL FUNDS

Mutual funds offer the small investor the advantages of professional management, convenience and liquidity, reasonable unit size, and diversification. Their drawbacks are loss of personal control and inability to take quick action because of transaction costs. Mutual funds can't switch heavily into cash and must diversify their investments, with no more than 5 percent in a single stock.

Mutual funds are open-ended investment management companies, in which the number of outstanding shares is not fixed.* They form large portfolios by pooling the resources of many individual investors. Among the hundreds of funds, each has a different investment objective or focus: funds that seek income, growth, or a balance; money market, international, bond, government securities, and specialty funds. Money market and international funds were touched on in Chapters 3 and 4, respectively. Bond funds will be described in Chapter 7, and government securities funds in Chapter 8.

The cost of fund shares is based on the fund's *net asset*

---

*There are also closed-end investment companies, which are more similar to corporations. These usually invest in the securities of other corporations, and their shares are traded on the market like corporate stocks.

No-load funds have no sales charges. They also are usually sold directly to the investor by mail and telephone, thus avoiding sales representatives' commissions. Both types of funds charge management fees. Other things being equal, then, you're better off buying a no-load rather than a load fund simply because you'll save the sales commission up front.

73

value (NAV), computed by dividing the total value of its assets by the number of shares outstanding. You purchase shares from the fund itself, which will also redeem your shares when you want to sell. In effect, mutual funds make a market in their own shares.

Load vs. No-load Funds

There are prevailing pricing arrangements for mutual funds: "load" and "no-load." Load funds charge a sales commission for executing a transaction, usually from 4 to 8 percent of the offering price. Commissions often apply only to the initial sale, but not to redemptions, and the percentage is reduced for larger purchases or for subsequent additional purchases ("rights of accumulation").

Unfortunately, recently things have gotten more complicated. Fund managers have developed new kinds of charges and special fees that can boost your annual costs to 2 percent or more of your holding. Some funds have also instigated or increased their rear-end loads—the fees charged when you withdraw your money from the fund. Be particularly cautious if your stockbroker is selling a 12b-1 fund with an annual distribution fee. The purpose of these fees is to cover brokers' commissions. They can vary widely, so be sure to compare them when you prepare to invest in a mutual fund.

Selecting a Mutual Fund

Sources of Information

Each fund publishes a *prospectus*, which is subject to approval by the Securities and Exchange Commission and must be quite comprehensive, including information on objectives and program, current holdings, financial statements, and directors. Most also publish annual reports.

In addition, there are several outside sources of information. Arthur Wiesenberger Services Corporation publishes a comprehensive summary of performance and other information, available through brokers or at large public libraries. Lipper Analytic Distributors, Inc. and *Forbes* magazine annually review mutual-fund performance.

Selection Criteria

In selecting a fund, the first criterion is that it match your investment objectives. You can probably find several funds that do. But your success depends on the fund's investment performance, and performance varies widely. Some funds consistently outperform the S & P's 500 Index by wide margins. In 1983, for example, stock funds overall gained an average of 20.2 percent; the S & P's 500 gained 22.6 percent, and the top-performing Oppenheimer Regency Fund gained 58.1 percent. The poorest performer that year, GSC Performance Fund, actually *fell* 19.4 percent. Yet both funds shared the same investment philosophy.

What this illustrates, graphically, is the need to compare a fund's track record and management thoroughly with that of competitors. Look at past performance in light of the fund's objectives. Try to learn something about the qualifications and experience of the portfolio managers. Examine the list of securities the fund invests in: if you were investing for yourself, would you want to own them or stocks like them?

Generally, you are best off buying a mutual fund that is part of a "family" of funds offered by the same managers. Usually, you will have no-cost privileges to transfer your money from one fund to another as your needs and economic conditions change. For example, in an economic expansion, a growth fund will do better than a balanced fund. The latter may do better in a declining market. When interest rates are high, a money-market fund may do better than either of the others.

What's important to me in a mutual fund is not what it does in a good year but how it performs over the cycle of four or five years. Does it preserve principal in a bad year? Many of them don't, and those are the ones you want to avoid. A mutual fund is a long-term investment, so be critical of long-term performance.

CHAPTER 6

STOCK OPTIONS

In the ten years since listed stock options were introduced by the Chicago Board Options Exchange, they have become available for over four hundred securities, with a sales volume greater than that of all the stock exchanges. Trading in options is a complex, high-risk business, and I don't recommend it for most investors. It should be left to the speculators and professionals.

However, because there are situations in which options can be used to provide insurance against large loss of capital for stock market investors, I will discuss them briefly and describe the situations in which you may be justified in using them as a protective device.

What Options Are

Any stock option is a right to buy or sell *100 shares of a particular listed stock,* called the underlying security, *at an agreed price,* called the exercise price or strike price, *by a specified date,* usually on a quarterly schedule of three, six, or nine months away.

The buyer pays the seller a sum of money, called the premium, for the right granted by the option. The buyer may then elect to exercise the option, resell it, or let it expire at the end of the allotted time. What you have when you buy an option, therefore, is a contract, rather than an equity interest as with an outright stock purchase or debt instrument like a bond.

Given their seemingly esoteric nature, why have options become so popular so quickly? One big reason is *leverage:* option buyers can play price moves in a given stock for a fraction of the cost of actual stock ownership. If they guess right, they make a potentially large profit from a relatively small investment.

Another reason is *limited and known downside risk.* The buyer's risk is predetermined; it cannot exceed the premium paid for the option. The seller's risks are different in nature, but can also be limited. A third reason is that options are more flexible than stock ownership, permitting the option trader to move more nimbly in response to the volatility that has characterized the stock market in recent years. And, of course, the existence of organized, exchange-based trading has greatly enhanced the liquidity of options.

The two types of options are known as calls and puts. A *call* option gives the buyer *the right to purchase a stock* at a future time for a fixed price. In exchange for the premium he receives, the call writer or seller agrees to sell his or her stock by a certain date for a fixed price. A *put* option gives the buyer *the right to sell a stock* by a future time for a fixed price. The put seller takes the premium and agrees to purchase the stock at any time, at the buyer's option, until a particular date for a fixed price. The put seller takes the premium and agrees to purchase the stock at any time, at the buyer's option, until a particular date for a fixed price. In either type of option, the difference is control: the buyer retains control, *while the seller forfeits control in exchange for the premium.* The buyer may sell or exercise the option at any time during its term (up to nine months). An option writer who is assigned an exercise must buy (put writer) or sell (call writer) on demand.

Option Premiums

What determines the price of an option? Several factors are involved.

The general price movement of premiums varies by the type of option. Since the option market is a competitive one, premiums will reflect overall supply and demand. When stock market prices are rising, more investors will want to purchase calls and fewer stockholders will choose to write calls on their stocks, preferring to hold them in hopes of further appreciation. Thus, the level of call premiums will tend to rise. At such times demand for puts is lower, and put premiums will, therefore, be lower also.

In a bear market, investors will want to purchase puts either for income or to protect themselves against losses, and put premiums will rise. The reverse applies to call premiums when stock prices are weak.

With respect to individual premiums, probably the most important aspect is the market value of the stock, with an option bearing a strike price closer to the current market value costing more than one further "out of the money." As the stock price moves in the direction of the strike price for the option, the premium value of that option will rise. Conversely, if the stock price moves further away from its strike price, the premium value will decline. Finally, the volatility of the underlying security is a factor, with stocks that fluctuate significantly (high betas) usually commanding higher premiums than those with stable prices.

A specific option price consists of two elements, its time value and its intrinsic value. The *time value* of an option is quite simple to understand since, in a sense, the option buyer is paying primarily for time. Thus, a 3-month option will be less expensive than a 9-month option with the same strike price. Or, to put it another way: since an option is a wasting asset having no value once it expires, the more time remaining until expiration, the higher the premium. The longer-term option is more valuable because of the greater likelihood that, during its term, the underlying stock will move in a direction that will permit the option holder to exercise or sell it at a profit.

Commissions

Commissions for options trades are generally considerably lower than those for stock trading. However, while the dollar amount is less, commissions typically comprise a larger *percentage* of the total investment. Since commissions vary among brokers and with the size of the transaction, they will be ignored in the examples in this chapter. Obviously, you cannot afford to ignore them in considering options transactions. They can affect your profits significantly.

Why People Trade In Options

We covered some general reasons for trading options early in the chapter: leverage, limited risk, and flexibility. Now let's examine in more detail how options can be used to achieve different investment objectives.

Why People Buy Options

People *purchase call options* if they think a stock will rise in price. (Similarly, selling puts is a bullish strategy, albeit a far more speculative one. See below.) For example, if XYZ is selling at $42 a share and you think it is underpriced, you can buy a 45 call for $2 a share. If the stock rises to $48 before your option expires, you've got a winner: you can either exercise your option and buy the stock now selling at $48 for $45, or you can resell your call option, which is now worth at least $3 plus its remaining time value, to someone else. The leverage aspect of the option transaction compared to an outright purchase of 100 shares of XYZ stock can be seen as follows:

	XYZ 45 Call	XYZ 100 Shares
Initial outlay	$200	$4,200
Sale price	$300	4,800
Gain	100	600
Percent return	50	16.6

The example disregards commissions in both cases. These are likely to be a higher dollar amount for the stock transaction than for the option, but a higher percentage of profit for the option transaction.

Even if you have enough available cash to purchase the stock outright, you may still wish to purchase the call option instead, investing the difference in a safe fixed-income security such as Treasury bills or notes. This protects you against the full impact of an adverse movement in the stock price while giving you the benefit of any favorable movement. In this case, you could invest $200 in your XYZ 45 call and the remaining $4,000 in a 6-month Treasury note at, say, 10 percent. You would then have an additional $200 in T-note income to partially protect you against a drop in the price of your stock or in the value of your option premium. Another reason for holding a call is to guarantee the price of a future stock purchase.

For example, you anticipate the availability of a lump sum of cash in several months and would like to purchase some QED shares. QED is selling at $31, but you expect it to rise significantly before your money becomes available. Buying a QED 30 call expiring at about the time when your funds will become available guarantees your ability to acquire QED near the current market price, regardless of any intervening appreciation. Whether or not this seems like a good deal depends on the option premium and your expectation of the magnitude of the stock's appreciation, among other factors.

Purchasing put options can be an excellent strategy for conservative investors by serving as insurance against a drop in the price of a security you own. I often recommend it for those who want to invest in common stocks with minimal risk. Your premium payment gives you the right to sell your stock for a specified price until the expiration date. The premium you pay for your "put hedge," as this kind of purchase is called, acts like an insurance premium: it ensures that your stock holding will not fall below the strike price for as long as the put goes out in time. If the stock declines during the term of the option, you still can sell it at your purchase price. Your only loss will be the premium you paid to acquire the option.

Buying a put hedge on an appreciated stock you already hold protects you against a decline in the stock price while still permitting you to partake in any further gains. Similarly, you can "insure" new stock purchases by purchasing a put option simultaneously when you buy the stock. This is known as "marrying the put." Consult your tax adviser for a more detailed explanation of the tax ramifications.

If you choose to write such an "insurance policy" on your stock, your maximum loss under any circumstances should be 8–10 percent. Yet you allow your potential for profit to remain unlimited. If you're willing to work with those odds, unlimited upside and 10 percent on the downside, then buy that insurance. Likewise, if you own a portfolio of stocks that have appreciated, you can protect your gains by buying a put hedge rather than a stop-loss order, where you may lose your holding unintentionally.

You can also *sell your put* hedge. If you have 100 XYZ at 18 and a $3 put, and XYZ goes down 8 points, that put you paid $3 for is now worth $11. So if you think there is no further downside risk on XYZ, you sell your insurance policy in a closing transaction for the higher price, make $800 on it, and still own the stock. By doing so, you make up the difference, so you've lost nothing. And you still own XYZ at $10, so you can wait for six months or a year and see if it goes back up to 18..

But if XYZ went down to 10 and you didn't sell your put, when the stock went back up to $18 *you wouldn't have made anything.* This is a good illustration of the crucial importance of keeping your wits about you when you deal options. This is no place for the lazy or inattentive investor.

Why People Sell Options

Selling calls on stock you already own is a very conservative strategy known as *writing covered calls.* If you sell a covered call, you collect a premium against the value of your stock in exchange for which you agree to sell your stock up to some future date (not more than nine months away) at a fixed price. Try to select stocks that don't fluctuate much or write a far out-of-the-money call so your chances of being assigned an exercise are minimized. You pick up additional income from the premium, which gives you another token of downside protection against loss. Some commonly used rules of thumb are that you should try to double your dividend income, or to generate an additional 20-percent yield from your stock portfolio.

The highest premiums tend to be generated by long-term, close-to-the-money calls. But these run a higher risk of being exercised. You must balance your premium income against the risk of loss of your stock. For instance, say you own QED stock at $20 a share, and you write a 25 call against it for a $3 premium. What you're saying is that if QED goes beyond $25, you're willing to have it called away from you. The call premium is just a means of collecting some more money while you own QED because you don't think it will go higher than 25. If it does go beyond 25, you are likely to lose it, because your call will be exercised.

There is a way to avoid being assigned an exercise. It is called a *closing purchase transaction*. In this instance it means you can *buy* a QED 25 call with the same expiration date, thus essentially buying back your option and canceling the original transaction. However, if the price of the underlying shares has risen above $25 (and hasn't already been exercised), the option you wrote will be worth more and buying it back at the going rate will probably cost you more than your call premium (plus additional commissions).

There's another catch: in exchange for the extra income of the premium, you're limiting your upside, and you have unlimited downside. In this example, if QED drops to $7 a share, you sell it for $7, and the premium has only protected you against the first $1 of that loss, or down to $19 a share. Not only that, but for your $1 premium, you're giving up the potential for $25 on up.

The difference between writing covered calls and buying put hedges, as forms of insurance, is control. If you write a covered call, you lose control. If the stock goes up, you can be sold out unless you execute a closing purchase transaction to nullify the original call. When you buy a put, you incur the cost of the premium, but *you* have control for however long that put goes out in time. If there is a decline in the stock market price after three months of a 6-month option, you can continue to hold the stock if you choose, because you're protected another three months, during which time the stock may rise in value.

Writing naked calls

This strategy consists of selling calls on stock you do not own. Its purpose is to derive premium income without undergoing the expense of purchasing the underlying security. (Brokerage firms do, however, have margin requirements for such transactions; these serve as collateral.)

If the stock price rises and such a call is exercised, the call writer would have to purchase stock in the market at a cost above the exercise price (not to mention commission charges) to make delivery on the contract.

Naked calls writing is extremely risky. Don't even consider it.

Writing put options

This is for people willing to speculate that the price of the underlying security will remain steady or increase during the term of the option. Its risks are similar to those of the uncovered call writer, and the motive of gaining premium income is also similar.

A variation on this strategy is to write cash-secured puts, in which the put writer deposits with his broker an amount equal to the option exercise price. This avoids the possibility of additional margin calls, and the broker can invest the cash in short-term instruments for the client.

Another purpose of put-writing is to try to acquire stock at a net cost below current value. In this case, the investor does not want to pay the current market price of $60 a share for QED stock. He writes a QED 60 put for a $5 premium per share. If the cost of the stock declines as expiration approaches, the option will be exercised.

The investor will acquire the stock at a "discount" of $5 a share, the premium income having offset his purchase cost by that amount. My feeling about this is that if you want to own a stock that has good value based on fundamentals, you should be willing to pay what the market says it is worth. Or you ought to have the patience to wait until a market correction drops its price a bit. The put-writing strategy is too indirect and has no guarantee of success. What if the price of QED drops to $45? You must purchase at a price way above market. Or, conversely, what if QED rises to $72? The put will not be exercised, and you have lost your opportunity to acquire the stock for $60 a share.

Index Options

In the past few years, options have become available on whole stock indices rather than only on the shares of a single company. They are now traded, for example, on the Standard & Poor's 500, the New York Stock Exchange Index, and the Value Line Index of 1,700 second-tier companies.

Options trading is flexible enough to serve a relatively broad range of investment objectives. The risky strategies are losers for most investors. Conservative option strategies, judiciously used, have a place in the prudent investor's portfolio. But, while no thoughtful person would be so foolish as to make an investment and then simply forget about it, options trading—even in its simplest forms—requires unusual vigilance. The wise investor must know himself well enough to determine whether or not he or she has the concentration, energy, or desire to be this attentive.

CHAPTER 7

BONDS

Whereas stocks represent an equity interest, bonds represent only a creditor position. As a bondholder, you are lending your money to finance the debt of the issuing entity. Thus, your degree of involvement with the issuer is more limited than that of the stockholder. You need be concerned only that the entity from which you purchase the bond has sufficient stability and liquidity to repay your principal and interest on time for the duration of the bond's term.

Most bond issues are offered in denominations of $5,000, by means of offering circulars that describe the financial condition of the issuer. In combination with data from the ratings services (see pages 90–91), these enable you to determine the relative degree of risk involved in a particular issue. Most bonds are sold in serial form, with portions of the issue coming due over a period of years.

Also unlike stocks, bonds are *fixed-income* securities. You know at the time of purchase precisely how much the bond will yield, and over what period of time. For some investors, this certainly is comforting, but there is no possibility of capital gains or earnings growth with bonds if they are held to maturity. What you see is what you get, and that has both advantages and drawbacks.

Risks of Fixed-income Investments

Any bond of reasonable quality will almost certainly make interest payments on time, and ultimately return your money intact. So it provides the most basic kind of safety; there is little or no risk of loss of principal *if* you hold the bond to maturity.

But there are exceptions even to this; bonds are not always as safe as they appear. For example, we warned our clients not to purchase bonds of the Washington Public Power System (now commonly known as WHOOPS) but many other investors were not so fortunate.

We know of one family in the Pacific Northwest who sold their family business, which they had spent a lifetime building, and placed $1 million—most of the proceeds—in WPPS Series 4 and 5 bonds. At the time the bonds were rated AA and AAA, and were paying 14 to 14½ percent tax-free yield. Figuring the family would receive $140,000 tax-free annual income, the father retired. Today, at age 66, he's back working as hard as he was thirty years ago because he has lost most of his principal. The bonds are probably worth 8 to 12 cents on the dollar. Their high ratings and guarantees were unwarranted. While such a major default is rare, it does point to the need for caution, even in the once staid bond market.

Depending on the nature of the bond and the size of the issuer, you may be subject to liquidity risk should you wish to sell your bond before maturity. For example, if after three years you need to sell your unrated 20-year bond to finance construction of the East Shadyville public parking garage, you may have difficulty finding a buyer. The larger the "float," or number of bonds issued, the more likely there will be a market for your bond. You should inquire of your broker as to whether the bond is listed (the secondary mar-

ket in bonds is exclusively over-the-counter, not on organized exchanges) and get his estimation of its liquidity.

Even more important than liquidity risk is interest-rate
risk. If interest rates have gone up during that period, your
bond will not be salable at its original price, or *par*. Instead,
you may be forced to sell it at a *discount*, because no one
will pay you the full face value of the bond if bonds of
equal quality are currently paying a higher yield. Discounting is a method of bringing the price of your lower-yielding
bond into alignment with current market conditions. On
the other hand, if interest rates have fallen in the interim,
a purchaser may be willing to buy your bond at a *premium*,
i.e., to pay more than par for your bond in exchange for its
higher yield.

Interest-rate risk has been significantly greater since 1979.
In that year, the Federal Reserve changed its focus from
controlling interest rates by adjusting the money supply to
controlling the money supply and letting interest rates vary
freely. Since then, interest rates have fluctuated widely and
rapidly and fixed-income long-term investments have become far less secure.

Even when you hold a bond to maturity, you can never
know for certain when you buy it what your money will
be worth in terms of purchasing power at that time. So
bonds, like all fixed-income investments, are subject to inflation risk.

Role of Bonds in Your Investment Portfolio

Your goal as an investor is always to maximize total return consistent with your tolerance for risk. For risk-averse
investors in the higher tax brackets, with a high need for
conservation of principal and current income, but relatively
little interest in capital accumulation (a combination which

frequently characterizes older investors), high-grade municipal bonds may be a suitable place for a relatively large
proportion of assets. Investors with higher risk tolerance and
a greater desire for capital appreciation will place a far smaller
proportion of their portfolios in bonds. Even for the latter
group, however, some high-quality bonds or bond instruments may be appropriate investments at certain times. In
the bond market, as in all investments, timing is crucial.

Taxes are another variable. For example, if your tax
bracket is 32 percent or less, taxable bonds may be suggested to you for their higher yield. But for any investor in
those brackets, bonds put you on the wrong side of the
investment street. You're banking that interest rates will stay
the same or drop, and that's not a good bet. Taxable bonds
are also a poor choice because when you get your interest,
it's taxed by the IRS, yet there is no growth potential whatsoever if the bonds are held to maturity. The exception is
to buy these bonds for a qualified plan, such as an IRA,
that shelters the income from taxation.

Bond Analysis and Rating Services

Two major agencies, Moody's and Standard & Poor's, rate
the relative safety of bonds. In rating a corporate bond, the
firms consider several factors, of which the most significant
are:

- The relation between earnings and interest
  charges, both level and trend
- The relation of long-term debt to equity
- The debtor's liquidity position
- The size and economic significance of the issuer

Credit-risk classifications range from prime (Aaa—
Moody's; AAA—S & P's) to very speculative or default (Caa,

Ca, and C—Moody's; CCC, CC, D—S & P's). Generally speaking, only the top three categories of each system are considered "investment"-grade. Lower-rated or so-called "junk" bonds may be suitable for some investors on a speculative basis.

Current Yield vs. Yield-to-Maturity

Bond yields are usually figured in one of two ways—current yield and yield-to-maturity. Current yield refers to the percent of annual return on the dollar amount paid for the bond, whereas yield-to-maturity is the total return the bond investor will receive on his purchase price by holding the bond until it matures. Since the coupon rate for a particular bond is fixed, the current yield will not change over the life of the bond. Yield-to-maturity, on the other hand, will vary, depending on whether the bond was purchased at par or at a discount or premium.

Types of Bonds

Let us examine in some detail the different types of bonds.

Taxable Bonds

Corporate bonds are debt instruments issued by a corporation to pay for major capital outlays like constructing a new plant. The company prepares an indenture, or deed of trust, which is its contract with the trust company that acts as trustee of the proceeds. Bonds issued by corporations are sold through investment bankers. Mortgage bonds are backed by company-held real property, whereas debenture bonds have no specific security behind them. If the corporation defaults, bondholders can foreclose its mortgage or force it into receivership.

Two features of which any corporate bondholder should be aware are call provisions and sinking funds. Most corporate bonds have a call feature within seven years or less, which permits the company to refinance its debt by calling bonds away from you. Since the company will obviously call its bond only if interest rates have gone down, this is a decided disadvantage to you as an investor. You will be forced to reinvest at a time not of your choosing and in a less desirable market. A sinking fund, on the other hand, is a positive feature. An issuer with a sinking fund pledges to set aside moneys regularly for the term of the bond issue to repay the principal of the bonds when they come due.

Government bonds are long-term obligations of the U.S. Government, and include Treasury bonds and U.S. Savings Bonds. They are generally considered to be among the most secure investments available, so they pay lower rates than most other bonds. Interest on these bonds is taxable as ordinary income. They are discussed in Chapter 8.

Tax-free Bonds

Municipal securities are the debt obligations of states and their local political subdivisions. The issuing of these bonds is the mechanism whereby these governmental units can raise money to finance public capital projects like water and sewer systems, highways, and school buildings, which cannot be paid for out of current revenues. This market is a substantial one, with a volume of new issues on the order of $100 billion a year.

The interest income from these securities is exempt from federal income taxes, so these issuers can borrow at lower interest rates than either corporations or the federal government itself—usually 35 percent lower than rates on comparable long-term taxable bonds. In most (but not all) states, obligations of the state itself and of local authorities within it are also exempt from state and local income taxes.

Two broad categories of municipal bonds are *general obligation* and *revenue* bonds. A general obligation bond pledges the full faith and credit of the issuing government for the repayment of the bond, while a revenue bond is backed only by the revenue anticipated from the facility to be constructed with the proceeds of the bond issue (e.g., a toll road or airport).

More recently, a third type of bond, the *industrial revenue bond,* has become quite popular. IRBs are issued by a public body, usually a municipal government, to provide construction capital at reduced rates for private for-profit corporations. They are backed by the credit of the private beneficiary rather than the issuer, and have been used to construct hotels and convention centers as well as industrial plants. The increasing use of IRBs, with their lower interest rates to the private debtor, has been criticized for funding a broad range of purposes not easily recognizable as being in the public interest. Their tax-favored status may become a victim of tax reform.

The range of issuers of tax-free bonds is broader than one may at first imagine. For example, local public-housing authorities issue bonds to finance the construction or rehabilitation of low-income housing projects. Under an agreement with the U.S. Department of Housing & Urban Development, PHA bonds are guaranteed by the U.S. Government. Public power authorities, school districts, and public hospitals are other examples of issuers of tax-free bonds.

Taxable or tax-free?

In choosing between a taxable and a tax-free issue, you need only three numbers: the yield of the taxable bond, the yield of the alternate municipal bond, and your top marginal tax bracket. Multiply the taxable yield by your tax bracket to determine your tax liability. Subtract that tax liability from the taxable yield to determine the after-tax yield. Unless the after-tax yield equals or exceeds the tax-free yield, buy the municipal.

Coupon vs. Zero-coupon Bonds

Most bonds in the past have carried coupons which were clipped and exchanged for quarterly or semiannual interest payments. In recent years, another form of bond has become increasingly popular. This is the zero-coupon bond, which is issued at a deep discount from its par value at maturity. Zero-coupons pay no periodic interest. Instead, the interest is compounded internally during the term of the bond and the full face value is paid at maturity.

Zero-coupon bonds are available in a wide range of maturities. You choose the maturity desired. The longer they go out the higher the yield (internal rate of return), and they just keep on multiplying and compounding. Thus, with a relatively small initial investment, you can accumulate a large amount of capital for a foreseeable future event like retirement or educational expenses.

Zeroes are appealing in part because of their apparent simplicity. You need not handle coupons or figure out how to reinvest your money frequently. But, like any other investment, zeroes do have some drawbacks.

First, there's no tax deferral with a taxable zero-coupon bond. For higher-income individuals, the after-tax return on taxable zeroes is poor. Individuals in higher tax brackets should not buy them, because even though you don't receive the income, you still have a taxable event. Year in and year out, you will be taxed on this "phantom income" that you don't receive.

Instead, higher-income investors should consider zero-coupon bonds or Treasury Bond Receipts (TBRs, a related zero based on U.S. Treasury bonds) *only* if the bonds are

placed in custodial account for a minor or for use in a qualified pension or profit-sharing plan, or in a Keogh or IRA.
Zero-coupons are useful in these cases because you can work
backward from the amount of principal you wish to have
at the end of the bond's term, and when you wish to receive it. As taxes are deferred under qualified plans and
reduced in custodial accounts, your dollars will grow at a
more rapid pace, depending on interest rates. You can build
maximum profit for payoff at a particular time for a particular need—such as college costs or retirement.

No investment these days is as simple as it seems, including zero-coupon bonds. Be cautious and do your homework. It is important to know something about both the
issuer and your broker. Be aware of the issuer's ability to
pay. Remember WHOOPS!

Tax-exempt zeroes are not suitable for most investors and
therefore are losers. They are wrong for everybody. Their
rate of return is deplorable, especially since they usually
have extremely long maturities (another disadvantage).

Yields may vary substantially. Compare yields on zero-
coupon bonds with approximately equivalent maturities
carefully to determine whether you are getting the best
available deal. A difference that may not seem like much
given the low initial payout may cost you dearly over the
life of the bond. Also be aware that most brokers advertise
bond yield before compounding, whereas banks advertising
competitive zero CDs usually quote an already compounded figure.

Similarly, sales commissions are not always competitive.
Insist that your broker quote commission charges separately, so you can see how much transaction costs will drag
down your net yield.

Another aspect to consider is the likelihood that you may
need to sell your zero before it matures. While all bond
prices decline when interest rates rise, the drop is more pre-

cipitous with zeroes because all the interest stays with the bond until it matures (rather than being paid out gradually, as with a conventional bond). For this reason, zeroes have shown wide swings in market since their introduction, and are less safe than they may at first appear.

When you buy a zero-coupon bond, the amount you will receive is guaranteed. You know exactly what you're going to get and when you're going to get it. As with any bond, the only thing you can't know is what the purchasing power of the money will be. With net returns currently around 10–12 percent, taxable zeroes can be an interesting investment for custodial accounts, qualified pension plans, and other tax-sheltered accounts. Like other bonds, though, they will sustain their long-term value and safety of principal only if interest rates stay constant or decline.

Forms of Bond Investments

Bearer vs. Registered Securities

Beginning in 1982, municipal bonds began to be issued primarily in registered form, in which the owner's name is recorded by the issuer and appears on the face of the bond. Interest is paid by check to the registered owner. Prior to that date, most municipal securities were bearer bonds, where the issuer has no record of the owner, who could collect interest from a paying agent, and transfer ownership merely by physically delivering the security.

Individual Bond Holdings

Unless you have a significant amount of money to invest, $100,000 or more, you may be ill-advised to purchase a single municipal bond, particularly in a small local issue. The reason, touched on earlier in the chapter, deserves reemphasis—marketability. If you hold a smaller amount of a particular issue and need to sell, dealers will offer a lower price per unit—so you lose. If you hold an obscure unlisted issue, they will offer a lower price—so you lose. As with used cars, it's a negotiated market—you buy retail and sell wholesale. Of course, there are exceptions: some bonds offer blue-chip security. Still, explore the possibility of investing in a bond fund or trust instead (see below).

How can you improve the odds? Look for insured or guaranteed bonds or PHA bonds, which are usually more salable. Don't be sentimental about small bond issues in your own community (or elsewhere); be certain the yield is high enough to cover higher expenses. And finally, don't put money into bonds at all if you expect to need it quickly. It is rarely advantageous to liquidate such an investment before maturity.

Unit Investment Trusts

These are fixed portfolios of municipal bonds that pay pro rata shares to the unit holders when the bonds mature. They lock in current rates, and are currently paying approximately 9 percent tax-free—that's net. Lots of young salespeople sell these hard to wealthy individuals who are looking for high yield. If you are in the 50-percent tax bracket, you would have to earn 18 percent on a taxable investment to match that return.

There is a catch: these are very long-term bonds, which won't mature for thirty or forty years. The value of the trust will remain constant only if interest rates are stable. If interest rates take off again and you have to sell sooner, it will be at discount, and you may lose a substantial proportion of your investment. Buy these only to lock in high rates when interest rates peak.

Tax-exempt Insured Trust

This is an attempt to build credibility with investors by using the trigger word "insured," and it sounds very good. But in fact it may be a loser. They're the same long-term bonds you find in a regular unit trust, and the same thing happens if interest rates go up. These trusts merely ensure that if the bond issuers are in default, your principal and interest will be paid *when due*. In other words, you will get your coupon payments twice a year, and your principal whenever the bond matures. But the default is *now*, not twenty-five years from now.

Bond Mutual Funds

These differ from trusts in that they are open-ended, so the fund managers can avail themselves of quick changes in interest-rate and credit conditions. They seek capital gains as well as income. Both the portfolio and the investors are constantly changing, and the fund has no specified termination date. Like unit trusts, bond funds usually have yields averaging ½ to one point below the market for individual bonds because of management costs. Their advantages are liquidity, reasonable safety, and convenience—important considerations for conservative investors.

Put Bonds

This is a new way to own municipal bonds. The bond, rated at least A, is bought at a discount and wrapped around an irrevocable letter of credit from a good, profitable bank or insurance company. The term of the put varies, but averages three years. You receive coupons for the interest during that time, but you are also guaranteed long-term capital gains. The institution promises to repurchase your bond *at par* annually during a two-week "window" around the anniversary date of your purchase, regardless of market conditions at that time. Put bonds have several advantages:

- The bonds are guaranteed, insured, highly rated, and safe.
- They are backed by a financial institution, and some may also carry certain government guarantees.
- They only tie up your capital for a few years.
- You are guaranteed redemption at par value.
- Maturities are flexible: 3, 6, or 8 years as you choose.

Put bonds help you adjust for the greater volatility in the bond market in these days of rapid swings in interest rates. The very unpredictability of financial conditions in general, including continuing deregulation and competition in the financial services industry, argues for more flexible financial management to take advantage of new opportunities as they arise. Put bonds, perhaps alone of bond instruments, permit that nimbleness.

Except for put bonds, most bonds are losers because they are less liquid, and their value may be eroded by inflation. Bond mutual funds are generally a better investment than unit trusts or insured trusts. Make certain your financial adviser is abreast of the fixed-income market and can help you invest when interest rates are high and get out when you should be out.

CHAPTER 8

GOVERNMENT AND GOVERNMENT-GUARANTEED SECURITIES

Long-term Government Obligations

These are the extremely safe familiar Treasury bonds and U.S. Savings Bonds. T-bonds are fixed-maturity securities of over ten years, guaranteed by the U.S. Government. Minimum denominations are $5,000 or $10,000. They are usually callable beginning five years before maturity. The yield on these bonds and other Treasury issues is the base from which the going rate on other securities is derived.

U.S. Savings Bonds are of two general types. Series E bonds were the first zero-coupon bonds. They are sold at a discount in denominations as small as $25, and pay their par value if held to maturity. You may also hold them beyond maturity, with interest rates set for ten-year increments based on the prevailing rates on extension.

Series H bonds are issued in denominations of $500 to $10,000 and pay semiannual interest. They are issued at par and mature in ten years. Series E bonds may be exchanged for H bonds, but not vice versa.

During the period of high interest rates in the late 1970s and early 1980s, U.S. Savings Bonds paid a very low rate

of interest and were considered almost laughable as investments. This is no longer true. The bonds are now pegged
to Treasury bill and note rates, so the rate of interest reflects
prevailing market rates. And, of course, their historic security remains unchallenged.

Government-guaranteed Securities

The U.S. Government guarantees other securities issued
by several government agencies. These federal guarantees
make the securities just about as safe as direct Treasury instruments, but because of their complexity, they usually offer yields up to 2 percent higher. This makes them of interest if your primary investment objective is income with safety.
Until recently, these securities were available only in very
large denominations, so they were accessible only to institutional investors, but most are now packaged with far lower
minimums. Interest received on these securities is fully taxable.

These issues are interest-bearing and have various maturity dates, as bonds do, and their value in the secondary
market drops as interest rates rise. Unlike bonds, they pay
out *both* interest and principal at stated intervals before
maturity. Thus, you do not get a chunk of money back
at maturity, as you do with a bond. The securities may also
mature long before their stated due date. Thus, you have to
figure out how to reinvest funds that come back to you in
uneven and unpredictable quantities, and the duration of
your investment may well be longer or shorter than you
anticipated. A closer look at the details of these securities
will help you understand why this is so.

GNMAs

The first agency to issue this type of security was the
Government National Mortgage Association (GNMA), be-

ginning in 1970. "Ginnie Mae," as it is called, is an agency of the federal government. What it sells are diversified portfolios of federally insured FHA (Federal Housing Administration) and VA (Veterans Administration) mortgages, with the same interest rates and terms, usually 30 years. Since late 1984, GNMA has also offered a security backed by adjustable-rate mortgages, with interest rates adjusted annually based on one-year T-bill rates (no more than a one-point change will be permitted in a given year).

The minimum share in a new pool of these mortgage-backed securities is still $25,000, but you can buy shares in older issues that have a smaller pool of outstanding mortgages for as little as $10,000. Also, brokerage firms repackage GNMAs into unit trusts or mutual funds sold in units of as little as $1,000.

Unit trusts assemble a portfolio that does not change over time, and usually carry a sales charge averaging 3.5 percent. The portfolios of Ginnie Mae funds can be adjusted by their managers as market conditions change. In any of these forms, your GNMAs are totally safe.

Since mortgages are often prepaid, the average life of a GNMA pool is twelve years. But you can't predict prepayment for any single mortgage pool; each will pay off at a different rate. Your pool could mature in less than twelve years, or longer. Obviously, prevailing interest rates have a lot to do with the likelihood of prepayment. If they drop, more homeowners will prepay their mortgages and refinance at the lower rates. If they rise, people are more likely to retain their lower-cost mortgages. There is an inverse relation between effective yield and the duration of the investment pool.

With Ginnie Maes *your income will be erratic,* because holders get both interest and principal as they are paid out, which is why these securities are also known as pass-through certificates. And your principal may come back to you at inconvenient times and in inconvenient amounts.

You may also find yourself out of your GNMA holding unexpectedly, with a reinvestment problem if interest rates are low. GNMAs are too volatile to be winners and, since most of the other government-guaranteed securities are modeled after GNMA, they may be losers, too.

FNMAs

The Federal National Mortgage Association (FNMA) is a congressionally chartered corporation rather than an actual government agency like GNMA. It issues securities similar to those issued by GNMA, but is backed by conventional mortgages. Known, inevitably, as "Fannie Maes," they work the same way and offer the same guarantee of interest and principal as Ginnie Maes. Their yields are usually slightly higher, and they consist of much larger pools of mortgages.

FHLMC

The securities of the Federal Home Loan Mortgage Corporation, known as "Freddie Macs," are also based on conventional mortgage loans. Their guarantee is slightly less golden that GNMAs or FNMAs; timely payment of interest is guaranteed, but if homeowners default or pay late, you will have to wait up to a year for that part of your money.

Like Fannie Maes, Freddie Macs are based on pools of several thousand mortgages. These larger pools make it easier to estimate the payback on the mortgages accurately, which is an advantage. But neither Freddie Macs nor Fannie Maes are the sole investment of any mutual fund or unit trust (although some funds have part of their money in this type of security), so the minimum investment in a new pool is still $25,000.

Collateralized Mortgage Obligations (CMOs)

This is another type of FHLMC security. Introduced in 1983, it provides a more predictable payment schedule. In exchange for the reduction in uncertainty, CMOs pay slightly lower yields than other pass-throughs.

In every CMO issue are mortgages with maturities of three to twenty years, divided into four classes. Within each class, all the mortgages have the same maturity. Investors in the classes with the three shortest maturities get semiannual interest payments, with *all* principal payments going first to the holders of the shortest-maturity class until they are fully paid off. Principal payments are funneled next to investors in the second-shortest maturity class, then to those in the third shortest. The minimum investment for any of these classes is $25,000.

Finally, holders of the longest-maturity CMO are paid off in a different manner; like zero-coupon bondholders, they receive their whole payment in a lump sum at maturity. These are available for as little as $1,000.

Student Loan Marketing Association

This is an agency of the U.S. Department of Education, and is known as "Sallie Mae." As the securities of the agencies described above provide a secondary market for mortgages, so Sallie Mae was created in 1972 to provide a secondary market for federally guaranteed student loans.

There are at least three ways to invest in Sallie Maes. Its bonds are just about as safe as Treasuries, but carry slightly higher yields. They are available in denominations of

$10,000. Sallie Mae's short-term floating-rate notes, issued for 6 months and paying about a third of a percent more than 3-month T-bills, are a good hedge against rising interest rates. Rates on the notes are adjusted weekly. Finally, you can buy Sallie Mae preferred stock, which has been traded on the New York Stock Exchange since 1983. Currently trading (April 1986) at around $51, its dividend is currently $3.17. It is considered a sound investment because of the continuing strong need for college loans.

A similar regional agency, the New England Education Loan Marketing Corporation, or "Nellie Mae," provides a secondary market for guaranteed loans issued in Massachusetts and New Hampshire. Its highly rated bonds mature in three years and are exempt from federal taxes. If you are a Massachusetts resident, they are also exempt from state and local taxes.

Other Government Securities

Other agencies of the U.S. Government also issue securities that do not carry government guarantees but are nonetheless considered extremely safe. These include the securities of the Federal Intermediate Credit Banks and the General Services Administration (minimum investment $5,000) and the Federal Land Banks (minimum investment $1,000). All pay interest semiannually, are noncallable, and are exempt from state and local taxes.

Similarly, international organizations supported in part by the U.S. Government issue their own securities, which are not tax-exempt. The securities of the World Bank and the InterAmerican Development Bank are of varying maturities and are issued in denominations of as little as $1,000.

The Government-Securities Market: A Note of Caution

Because of the phenomenal increase in the federal deficit and the national debt, the Treasury has been forced to issue an ever greater amount of new securities. Bidding directly in government auctions and helping Uncle Sam find buyers for that debt are thirty-six "primary" dealers who trade directly with the Fed. In exchange for this privilege, they submit to relatively minimal federal reporting and oversight requirements. In 1981, the primary dealers traded $25 billion worth of government securities a day. In 1984, they traded *$60 billion a day!*

In addition, there is a far larger number of minor dealers in the secondary market who trade a small proportion of the total volume. Remarkable as it may seem, this market is essentially unregulated by either the government or the dealers themselves. In the absence of formal margin requirements, the dealers and their customers (mostly institutional investors) can use leverage of as much as 50:1 to bet on the direction interest rates will take. Bond futures and futures options are a big part of this game. When you lose, you lose big.

Another key mechanism used by government-securities dealers are repurchase agreements. These so-called "repos" are short-term loans backed by government securities as collateral. The borrower is usually a securities dealer who pledges to buy back the repo at a higher price and hopes to trade with the proceeds at enough of a profit to offset more than his costs. But the securities collateralizing the loan may be pledged to more than one borrower. This is analogous to variable hedging with options. It may be a losing proposition for the investor.

So far, there has been no major problem among the primary dealers. But a number of the smaller dealers have bet wrong. When interest rates rise, the value of the securities underlying their repurchase agreements falls. Since the repos are often undercollateralized in the first place, and the dealers' trades are highly leveraged, several of them have failed.

Too often they have dragged with them relatively unsophisticated smaller investors like school districts and thrift institutions. Thus, the crisis among the Ohio and Maryland savings and loans when one minor dealer, ESM, went into bankruptcy.

Individuals with large amounts of capital may be asked if they would like to purchase repos. This is an increasingly dangerous game, offering none of the safeguards of direct purchases of Treasury securities. Unless you are comfortable as a speculator and you know your dealer's credentials are impeccable, skip it until the inevitable day when reasonable regulatory controls have been established.

Government securities are the epitome of safety, but the tradeoff is relatively low yields. The yield and return of principal on most government-guaranteed securities are unpredictable. Each for its own reasons may be an investment loser. Professionally managed government-securities portfolios, on the other hand, have notably higher yields (12 percent as of mid-1985) and excellent safety for long-term investors. For the moment, they are investment winners.

CHAPTER 9

INSURANCE

M ost people hate insurance. They hate paying the premium, they hate trying to understand it, which they don't, and they hate pulling out the policy and trying to understand it, which they can't. Yet the principles underlying insurance are sound; for many purposes it is a necessary expenditure. So despite our distaste, we keep buying insurance anyway. And certain tax advantages of insurance form the basis for some of the most appealing low-risk investments.

Risk Management

Insurance is simply one form of *risk management*. Risk management recognizes and acknowledges various forms of risk or exposure, estimates their magnitude and likelihood, and then attempts to control them. Several categories of control are possible—risk avoidance, risk reduction, risk assumption or retention, and risk transfer.

For example, if you are an employee of a company, you have some risk (which varies with the individual and the company, and over time) of losing your job. The management of this risk may consist of doing the best job you can and staying on good terms with your boss (risk avoidance), keeping your résumé updated and remaining in touch with other firms that may have need of your services (risk reduction), having liquid savings equal to at least three months' after-tax income (risk assumption), and participating in an unemployment compensation program (risk transfer).

Many risks are either relatively insignificant or uninsurable. In deciding which risks to insure against, you make a rough mental calculation of the total amount at stake in relation to your total wealth. For instance, the relative value of your home and its contents is probably so high in relation to your total assets that its loss could wipe your family out financially. Therefore, you decide to insure your home against fire and smoke damage. But if your teenage son drives a ten-year-old clunker, you may decide to forgo purchasing collision (not liability) insurance for the car because its relative value is too low to be worth the cost (even though the risk of your son's having an accident may be relatively high).

Insurance is a means of reducing the financial burden of certain risks by dividing the losses among many individuals. The premium for the insurance protection is the amount you choose to pay in exchange for shifting most of those risks with potentially catastrophic consequences to others, reducing them to financially manageable size. This is known as the "large-loss principle." The decision is based not on the likelihood of the risk but on its severity should it actually occur. The use of deductibles or co-insurance can usually cut the expense of insurance coverage significantly, without substantially raising your exposure.

Choosing an Insurer

Your decision should be based on four factors: the company's financial soundness, the quality of its service, the types of coverage offered, and its prices. These may seem obvious, but can, in fact, be difficult to determine with accuracy. In determining financial soundness, special accounting techniques used for insurance companies make the company's asset size an unreliable indicator. The policy-holder's surplus ratio, which compares net worth with liabilities, will give you a more useful basis for comparison. Best's Reports provide detailed descriptions and financial data on insurance companies, plus a rating service analogous to S & P's or Moody's for bond issuers. Price considerations should always be secondary to the company's record of financial safety. The quality of claims service often depends on the agent or broker; try to find an experienced one whose reputation of assistance to clients is sound. And be sure to enlist the agent's help on a continuing basis as your insurance needs change.

Life Insurance

Life insurance indemnifies against the economic risk of premature death. Its liquidity can be especially important if most of your estate is in assets such as a house or small business. It may be available at low group rates, through either your employer or organizations to which you belong, without evidence of insurability. The three main types are term, whole-life, and universal life.

Deciding How Much Insurance You Need

One approach adds up what your dependents will need in the event of your death, lump-sum expenses (e.g., funeral costs and college tuitions), readjustment costs (such as selling a home and moving), life income for the spouse, income for dependent children, retirement needs, and other special needs, if any. Then see what proportion of the need will be met by Social Security or other benefits; increase your coverage, if necessary, to meet the rest.

The human-life value approach is based on the loss of

earnings to the family if the insured were to die, estimated annual average earnings from now until retirement, net of taxes and your individual expenses, multiplied by some discount factor to reach a net present value. A simpler formula calls for three to five times current salary, depending on the amount of capital on hand (to avoid liquidating assets to meet final expenses and taxes).

Term Life

Term insurance provides only protection, for a specified period of time and a relatively low annual premium for young people. Term is especially appropriate for families with young children. The lives of both parents should be insured, because even if one does not work, replacing his or her household and child-care services would be a major expense to the surviving wage earner.

The two kinds of coverage are level-term, a contract with a specified amount of insurance for the entire period, and declining-term, in which the amount of coverage gradually decreases.

If you are young and need protection, the cheapest and most appropriate choice is term insurance. When more expensive forms of coverage are suggested, ask the agent why you shouldn't buy less expensive term protection and invest the difference you save in high-yielding tax-advantaged annuities or municipal-bond funds.

However, older people will find term life increasingly expensive; other means of protection may be more appropriate for them.

Whole-Life

This is protection for one's whole life, at level annual premiums, combined with a savings or "investment" plan.

Part of the premium provides a death benefit, and the rest is invested on your behalf at a relatively low rate of interest. Traditionally, the client was not told the rate of interest or the earnings on his policy. Over a long period of time, the buildup in cash value replaces the insurance protection until (at around age 100), the policy is "paid up."

The insurance policy is personal property and can be assigned to others. Usually, there is a policy-loan provision that enables the policyholder to borrow up to the cash value of the policy at below-market interest rates, beginning after the third year of premium payments. Any amount not paid back before the holder's death is subtracted from the proceeds to beneficiaries. A number of *riders* are available to add different types of coverage to your whole-life policy, such as disability-income benefits or declining-term insurance. The policy may also pay dividends, depending on the investment experience of the company's portfolio, which can be used to offset part of the premium cost or reinvested with the insurer.

Settlement options in the event of the insured's death usually include an interest option, whereby the insurance company holds the proceeds at a guaranteed (low) rate of interest; fixed-amount option, which provides a stated monthly income until the proceeds are exhausted; fixed-period option, in which the period of payout is fixed and the proceeds vary; life-income options, which involve the purchase of an annuity; and joint and last-survivor options, in which the payout is spread over two beneficiaries' lifetimes.

Universal Life

Universal life was created by people in the industry who felt that insurance people for years had been ripping off their clients by selling them whole life. Universal life combines term insurance and investment built around the tax benefits of a traditional insurance contract, but modernized and improved. The insurance contract offers safety and tax-free accumulation of income. During the time that whole-life policy premiums are building up cash value, the gain is not taxable to the policyholder. Unlike an annuity, it is not tax-deferred. Rather, properly done, it may be tax-exempt.

Universal life takes advantage of this "inside buildup" feature of insurance, also. But rather than paying 3 to 5 percent like whole-life, universal life guarantees gross returns that are much closer to prevailing market rates. Yet there is still no risk of loss of principal—you have a binding contract. Universal life is not only protection for the individual with a side fund, but also an investment that is competitive with current investment rates. Of course, while yields can go up, they can also decline.

Like other life insurance, any death benefit does not have to go through probate and is not taxable to the beneficiary. These are significant benefits for retirement and estate planning.

Universal life policies are far more *flexible* than traditional whole-life policies. For example, they permit the purchase of additional protection (not usually permitted with whole-life policies). They allow the policyholder to pay in larger or smaller premiums at his option, rather than requiring a level premium. And some policies even have cost-of-living increase options.

While universal life reduces costs by not paying high commissions to sales agents, it does have costs to the insured. One advantage of universal life policies is that they provide full disclosure of fees and interest buildup to the policyholder in an annual report.

These payments may substantially reduce the advertised rate of interest on your policy during the first few years. If your insurer advertises a no-load policy, make sure that it doesn't have high surrender charges, or "back-end loads," if you withdraw your funds within the first few years.

Some holders of whole-life policies may wonder why they should consider a switch. Why not borrow out the cash value of their policies? One reason is that most older whole-life policies are obsolete in other ways. The actuarial tables say that people are living longer, that the premiums should go down, and the protection can go up. People who take out the cash value of their insurance policies are doing half a job, like hitting a single instead of a home run.

Variable Life

These policies let you direct where your policy's cash values will be invested, usually in one of several mutual funds with different objectives. The death benefit will carry a guaranteed minimum with such a policy, but could go higher if the investment program is very successful. When you consider variable life, consider as an alternative whether you should simply buy term insurance and invest the difference, if you intend to direct the investment anyway.

Insurance-based Tax Shelter Plans

This is a special version of life insurance for higher-income people. This modified whole-life insurance plan with tax-shelter aspects is offered by brokerage firms under proprietary names like OMNI, DynaPlan, Omega, and Ultraplan. It uses the deductibility of policy-loan interest and the tax-free inside buildup features of conventional life insurance to create a low-risk tax shelter. You pay a larger premium for a smaller death benefit, and the broker takes a smaller commission, so more money is left for investment. Cash value builds up much more quickly than with traditional whole-life policies. For the first several years, the accumulation phase, you pay a large annual premium. Depending on how much you want to shelter, you can put in any amount. If you are an owner of a service or professional corporation, you may not have to fund the initial contributions, as there may be benefits to the corporation in providing you with insurance protection. Check with your firm's tax adviser.

Next, you receive a nontaxable refund of your equity in the plan to date. In the third phase, you borrow money against the policy's cash value, using tax-qualified policy-loan interest to generate deductions far in excess of out-of-pocket costs. Properly planned, this can yield a stream of deductions to shelter other income.

The deductibility of policy-loan interest is the "seed" of a tax shelter, but most life insurance contracts grow too slowly to borrow much more than the amount required to pay the premium (minimum-depositing). For each $1 in interest, they generate $1 in deductions. This new breed generates write-offs of 5 to 1 or better, with no market risk.

This is an investment gem for sheltering assets from an IRA, Keogh, pension plan, profit-sharing plan, sale of a business, etc. If you are building up tax-deferred principal in your IRA or Keogh, you will face a tax problem when it comes out. You can either *pay the tax* or have it *come out tax-free*. This concept is the only way to do the latter. If you're planning to sell your business and retire, if you're getting a distribution from the sale of limited-partnership assets—whatever your form of income—you can avoid taxes on the income with the stream of tax write-offs from a tax-shelter plan designed for you. Despite its complexity, this is a low-risk, high-flexibility tax-shelter investment.

The plan has one negative: you can implement it today, but it takes time to receive the benefits. You must pay in contributions for a period of time before receiving a tax-free refund. *If* you can plan four to seven years ahead, you can set up a stream of guaranteed tax deductions and write them off for the rest of your life without risk, reducing or eliminating your tax liability. The stream of tax deductions will build up so you will have totally predictable tax write-offs every year.

Let's walk through an example. Assume a first-year contribution of $10,000 and similar contributions for the next six years. The total investment is $70–75,000. At the end of seven years, 90–100 percent of this investment comes back tax-free as return of capital. Thus, you have *nothing at risk*, nothing on the table. Then for the rest of your life or that of your beneficiaries, the plan generates a stream of tax benefits, in this case totaling up to $350,000 worth of deductions (the average is 500 percent of capital invested, depending on your age).

There is no investment risk, no tax preference or recapture of any kind. Everyone is different, but if you are able and willing to plan ahead and you anticipate significant income, you will want to reduce or eliminate the tax liability on that income. This unique and specialized investment is one very effective way to do it.

Health and Disability Insurance

As with life insurance, the best benefits may be available to you through your employer or another group of which you are a member. Medical and hospital costs are soaring, and it is foolhardy to risk a catastrophic loss by failing to insure against both sickness and accident expenses.

Disability Insurance

You are far likelier to suffer partial or total disability before retirement age than to die young. Yet, many income earners neglect to insure themselves against this possibility, which could have extremely adverse consequences—including not only the loss of income but the cost of caring for the disabled individual as well.

The sources of disability coverage include Social Security and state worker's compensation benefits, but these are not complete. Social Security is useful only for long-term total disability. Worker's compensation does not provide 24-hour-a-day coverage, but applies only to occupational or work-related accidents or diseases.

The disability-income feature of your group health insurance may be your best protection. Key features in any policy are the definition of disability used, the maximum-benefit period, and the waiting or elimination period. Disability may be defined as the inability to engage in any gainful occupation (a very narrow definition), or in terms of inability to work in one's own or a similar occupation (a more liberal definition). Most group health insurance plans provide some coverage for short-term disability income. Somewhat fewer protect against the more serious risk of long-term disability with benefits based on a percentage of earnings, a relatively high maximum monthly benefit, and a longer maximum-benefit period. Most such policies have a coordination-of-benefits provision to avoid duplicating other coverage.

If your employee benefits do not include long-term disability coverage or you do not have access to such coverage through some other group, consider purchasing individual insurance to guard against this very hazardous exposure. Note that an "own occupation" definition should apply for as long a period as possible to best protect you. The policy should have twenty-four-hour coverage and be noncancelable or guaranteed renewable until retirement age. If the premiums seem prohibitive, analyze how long you could manage on other resources (including your liquid emergency fund) and find out how much you can reduce the cost by extending the elimination period. You may be able to add a disability-income rider to an individual life insurance policy for less than a separate policy would cost.

Medical Expense Insurance

If you are over sixty-five, you are entitled to Medicare coverage. Otherwise, your coverage will again most likely be through your employer.

These benefits may either be provided on a service basis, as with Blue Cross–Blue Shield, or on an indemnity or reimbursement basis up to a certain limit, as with most insurance company plans. Basic benefits usually cover hospital expenses such as room and board and general nursing, other hospital services, and surgical benefits, among others, up to a specified dollar amount. Major medical and comprehensive coverages pick up where basic coverage leaves off to protect against catastrophic medical expenses. They usually have a deductible and co-insurance provision, which means that the insured is liable for paying a constant proportion of any expenses incurred. They also have a maximum-payout limit.

Both the basic and major medical types usually cover the insured employee and any dependents. Generally, if you leave your job, your coverage terminates immediately (no grace period); but conversion privileges may apply—usually at a higher monthly premium.

In either group or individual health insurance, preexisting conditions—illness or injury you already have when you buy the policy—may not be covered. However, this provision is subject to a "time limit on certain defenses," which essentially means that this right of the insurer expires after the first two or three years of the contract.

Property and Liability Insurance

This takes care of the last major category of risks: the risks of loss or damage to personal property, and the risk of liability for damage done on or with your property. These risks could wipe out the assets you have invested, or hoped to invest.

Property and Auto Insurance

While these are a necessary expense for any conscientious person, they are not technically a form of investment and will not be covered here. Make sure your policies are adequate (including replacement costs), up-to-date, but not excessive. Experts in insurance will be delighted to answer your questions about coverage and costs.

Liability Insurance

Obviously, your homeowners and auto insurance policies protect against some of the most significant categories of liability exposure, such as a car accident you cause. Comprehensive personal liability (CPL) insurance protects against legal obligations to pay for bodily injury and medical payments arising therefrom, or for property damage sustained on your premises or on account of your personal property. Given the size of awards in some negligence liability cases in recent years, you may also consider purchasing an "excess liability" or umbrella policy to pay and defend against liability claims beyond the limits of your CPL protection.

You may be subject to other exposures, depending on your personal situation. If you employ domestic help or occasional household workers, your state may require you to carry worker's compensation insurance. If you serve on the board of a corporation or condominium association, you may need a director's and officer's liability policy. If you own investment property, you must insure the property itself and carry liability coverage as well. You may also need additional coverage for business or professional pursuits, depending on the nature of your work. This can be quite costly and complicated, and is beyond the scope of this book.

No personal financial plan can be considered complete without risk management to protect against loss-producing hazards that could ruin your carefully laid plans. In addition, in the case of life insurance, there are investment aspects to consider. Whatever your situation, review your insurance coverage regularly to assure that it is still adequate and appropriate.

CHAPTER 10

ANNUITIES

Annuities are winners. They are for people who want a financial investment that offers safety of principal if carefully and properly bought, that permits them to accumulate money on a tax-deferred basis, to complement Social Security (which is held together with Scotch tape anyway) and other long-term money. If you are such a person, you can use an annuity to build a side fund with confidence, one that will give you the freedom to retire when you want to.

What we call "life" insurance is a misnomer; it would be more accurate to call it death insurance. An annuity is truly *life* insurance; it guards against the possibility of outliving one's income. The payout schedule of an annuity is based on standard mortality tables. But even if you live beyond your life expectancy, the mortality guarantee in your contract means that your payments will continue throughout your lifetime.

The concept has been around a long time, perhaps forty or fifty years. People in the nonprofit sector—schoolteachers and administrators, college professors, hospital administrators, even government figures like presidents and congressmen—have been involved in annuities going back to World War II and before. This is the tax-sheltered annuity (TSA) for retirement income, discussed in Chapter 14.

Characteristics of Annuities

The key word with most annuities is *safety*. Both principal and interest are guaranteed. An individual who is not currently using all his or her liquid assets puts in a principal amount that accumulates tax-deferred. At 8 percent interest, it will double in nine years; at 12 percent, it will double every six years. At that rate, if you start with $50,000 and plan to retire in twelve years, you know that in the worst case, you will have $200,000 available when you retire. This amount can be paid out to you as lifetime income, or to you and a beneficiary of your choice.

The annuity concept is one of the best ways to build a side fund of your own for retirement. Interest accumulates tax-free. Usually the income is guaranteed for your life, and, cumulatively, it greatly exceeds your initial capital sum. An annuity is also a useful place to roll over a lump-sum distribution from a pension or profit-sharing plan.

Is there any appreciation on these? Just the benefit of the compounding effect and no drain of any taxes as you go along. At 12 percent, $100,000 will be $200,000 in six years. You never pay tax on the internal return under the federal exemption on inside buildup.

The objective, while you are in your highest earning years and thus your presumably highest tax bracket, is to let your money accumulate tax-deferred. When you retire, you're supposed to be in a lower bracket, so you pay the taxes on the withdrawals then. What it will be worth in terms of command over dollars or purchasing power is the real question. Also, you can shelter the profits when they come out, as discussed in the last chapter.

Most annuities provide some liquidity; you may remove your funds at will. However, there are now fairly severe tax consequences for early withdrawal, plus insurance-company penalties during the early years of the contract (see section on tax aspects, p. 126). If the interest rate falls below the guaranteed rate on your annuity, a "bailout" provision permits you to surrender the contract without charges. Your annuity may also be exchanged for another contract without having to pay tax on the accrued interest. If you die before the end of the guaranteed payout period, your estate receives the proceeds of an annuity immediately, which avoids probate.

Types of Annuities

Immediate annuities begin paying income right away, whereas *deferred* annuities do not start paying out until some future date. Because the earnings are not taxed until payout, they can accumulate faster under a deferred annuity. Immediate annuities are always purchased with a single premium, but deferred annuities may also be purchased on an installment basis.

The amount of payment may be fixed or variable. *Fixed* annuities guarantee principal, interest rate, and payout. The income from a *variable* annuity will depend on the value of the investment portfolio funding the annuity. People choose variable annuities, which invest primarily in equities, in hopes of hedging better against inflation than the fixed-dollar securities in which fixed annuities are invested. In exchange for this possibility of greater appreciation, they take greater investment risk, although the annuity will still make lifetime payments (the *size* of the payments is unknown with a variable annuity).

A retirement annuity pays income for life, with (if you choose) a guaranteed minimum of either ten or twenty years. If the annuitant dies before that date, most annuity contracts obligate the insurer to pay the remainder of the investment, up to the minimum guaranteed return stipulated in the contract, to his or her beneficiary. You may also choose a "joint and last survivor" annuity, which provides a specified income over the lifetimes of two individuals (yourself and your spouse, for example). But you will pay a higher premium for the same monthly payout. Besides life annuities, you may also choose payments for a designated period, or payments for a particular dollar amount.

Combination Annuities

Some people are looking for immediate income because they need it. One new product that can, provide it is the combination annuity. Since 1982, if you take money out of an annuity, the first money out is your interest (see tax section on page 126)—*except* when you buy an immediate annuity. This investment concept, the combination annuity, takes advantage of that fact and combines two different annuities. Not only do you have guaranteed yield and safety of principal, but you also have an investment that will immediately start paying income, much of it tax-benefited.

The formula is to divide the principal amount of the annuity into two contracts. The first contract is an immediate annuity that pays you the income from years one to five. The second annuity you buy is a five-year deferred annuity, which offers your principal back after five years. You can choose any of the usual payout options to receive the income from this contract: a rollover into another annuity, gradual payout (taxable), or conversion to an immediate annuity.

Suppose you're in a 25- or 30-percent bracket and you paid $100,000 for a combination annuity. At 11.5 percent, you get $11,500 a year of annuity income. About $9,500 will be tax-exempt for the first five years. The reason is that part of your contract is an immediate annuity. For the immediate annuity portion, you are assumed to be withdrawing part principal and part interest. As you withdraw it, the interest is taxed, but the principal is not. So your annual income tax in the first five years would be under $1,000.

Meanwhile, the death benefit and cash value are accruing to ever higher levels throughout the contract. So your $100,000 today gets you a guaranteed annual income for five years, much of it tax-benefited, and still gives you your principal back at the end of five years in whatever form you choose. So you have a high net rate of return for five years, you'll get all your money back at the end, *and* you have all these tremendous tax advantages throughout. This is a very sophisticated and unique method for creating tax-advantaged income.

For those of you receiving Social Security, if you file an individual tax return and if you have over $25,000 in total income according to the formula, or, on a joint return, $32,000 of income, you may have to refund some of the Social Security benefits. The Social Security payments were taken from you for so many years and put in the system; you were paid no interest. And now, if you live long enough, Uncle Sam returns them to you not only with no appreciation whatsoever, but substantially devalued by inflation. Now the income may also be taxed! The only way you can avoid this legally is to buy a combined annuity or other investment where the income is exempt from the formula on Social Security benefits.

The Bad Apple

You may recall the widely publicized financial collapse of Baldwin-United, once the second-largest seller of annuities. No investor lost his capital, but that does not compensate for the major inconvenience and emotional strain imposed on Baldwin-United investors, and the confusion and panic engendered among investors in general.

Years earlier, a man who had purchased a very large

Baldwin-United annuity attended one of my investment seminars. He raised his hand and asked me when he should get out. I said "yesterday," and he got out immediately. As it turned out, he got his money back literally the day before their assets were frozen.

Let me emphasize that this is neither the behavior pattern nor the reputation of most companies in this field. But it does highlight the need for caution and good advice when selecting an annuity. The broker or adviser you deal with is the most crucial element, the one-on-one contact between you—the client—and the insurance company.

Tax Treatment of Annuities

At one time, annuities were a useful device for people of high income who needed a short-term tax shelter and could afford large lump-sum payments. Withdrawals were taxed on a first-in–first-out (FIFO) basis, meaning that you were assumed to be withdrawing your own principal first. Thus, much of the income could be sheltered from taxation. Annuities were also used to provide income for minors—during college years, for example.

These uses have become much less appealing due to 1982 and 1984 tax law changes. Under current law, withdrawals are taxed on a last-in–first-out (LIFO) basis, so you are taxed at ordinary income rates on the interest *first*. Also, a tax penalty of 5 percent now applies for withdrawals before you reach age 59½, even if no insurance-company penalties apply. Both changes have reduced the liquidity of annuities. While annuities serve as well as ever for retirement income since these changes were implemented, their utility for a broader range of objectives is just about gone.

Another change applies to the distribution of the annuity proceeds at death. If your beneficiary is your spouse, the tax deferral may be continued even before the payout period. However, if someone else is your beneficiary, the person must either apply the cash value to a life annuity within one year or take complete distribution within five years. These rule changes apply to contracts purchased after January 18, 1985, but not to those owned before that date.

If you own a single premium-deferred annuity purchased prior to August 13, 1982, you can withdraw up to the original amount invested tax-free because, before that date, the first moneys out were considered nontaxable returns of principal; the interest stayed in the reserve.

How to Shop for an Annuity

Fees and charges for annuities vary considerably, and so do the actual interest rates you receive. The insurance company is likely to have a stable of mutual funds that it invests in. Look for switching privileges among those funds that will enable you to move your money when market conditions change.

If you need to withdraw your funds in the first several years, you will pay the company a "surrender charge." The percentage ranges from 1 to 7 percent, and may decline gradually over a number of years or apply at a constant rate for the first five or six years only. The number of years this charge applies also differs from one company to the next, making it worth your while to comparison shop. (These fees are in addition to the IRS penalties.)

So the advantages of an annuity under the existing (1985) tax code are that it will grow on a tax-deferred basis, safely and predictably. If you have a qualified IRA or Keogh, there is no conflict in having a single premium-deferred annuity in addition, because it's out of your own pocket. When you do pull it out, you will have tax liability, but you will have had two important benefits: (1) the use of the money to compound for you, not for the IRS; and (2) payment of taxes in your lower retirement tax bracket. It's a great tool for financial planning in general, and also for estate planning because it passes to your survivors free of probate.

CHAPTER 11

GOLD, PRECIOUS METALS, AND GEMS

Always treasured, gold has a mystique that goes back thousands of years. Mankind universally considers the substance rare, precious, and exotic. Many cultures regard gold as the safest and most portable form of wealth, as in the coin jewelry worn by Middle Eastern women. In politically troubled regions around the world, people think of gold as "flight capital" that will retain its worth wherever they may go if they are forced to flee their countries.

Gold concentrates great intrinsic value in relatively little volume and weight. Because of these qualities, most of the gold mined throughout history is still traceable and half of all known gold is held by governments and central banks as a reserve asset.

But does all this make gold a winning investment for you today? Perhaps, and perhaps not.

I look upon gold essentially as an insurance policy to offset possible losses in the value of your other investments. Gold has an awesome record of stability in purchasing power that extends over centuries. It maintains or increases its value even—or perhaps especially—in precarious economic times. When inflation is high and cash investments are losing value, gold is likely to appreciate substantially. Because gold behaves differently from other asset categories, it can act as a stabilizing element, helping to balance your overall portfolio and to preserve your capital.

Sometimes I am perplexed by the way many people think. We insure our lives because we want our beneficiaries and loved ones to be taken care of. We insure our home because it's usually our major tangible asset. If there's a burglary, fire, or some other catastrophe, we want at least partial protection. We insure our cars because if someone steals them or plows into them we want to recover the loss. Why not insure some of our liquid assets? Surely that is equally logical and sound. Yet many people fail to consider the possibility of doing so.

Is there total safety in gold? Certainly not. No one investment can provide total safety. But seen as a hedging device, gold has a place in the prudent individual's portfolio. On the other hand, people who sink all their money into gold are as unwise as those who keep all their money in S & Ls or buy only Treasury bonds.

To me, gold is one of today's sleepers as a possible investment opportunity. While inflation remains relatively low and the dollar relatively high, gold prices should stay low, making this a good time to buy for the long term. But I am very sensitive to varying emotional and psychological tolerances for risk, and I know this suggestion is by no means appropriate to everyone's needs. For those of you who have most of your portfolios in place, and can tolerate the uncertainty in day-to-day gold prices, I would suggest having some gold as a long-term hedge against inflation.

Characteristics and Risks of Gold Investments

Gold prices are tremendously sensitive to people's levels of anxiety about world economic conditions and political instability. Further, over 60 percent of the world's gold is mined in either South Africa or the Soviet Union, and both countries stockpile gold for sale at times of their own choosing. Thus, its value is more volatile and its trading more subject to international upheavals than those of more liquid assets. Gold can and has risen astronomically, as it did for several years in the late 1970s, but it can also fall dramatically, as it has in the years since.

The possibility of extensive government regulation is one risk of owning physical metals. Beginning during the Depression in 1933, Americans were legally prohibited from buying gold as an investment for forty years, until permissive legislation was enacted in the mid-1970s. The U.S. Government classifies silver and platinum as strategic metals for national defense, and arguably might take over private stores in a military emergency.

Liquidity used to be a problem with gold. Since investment gold was legalized, it has become increasingly acceptable as a legitimate investment medium. The liquidity of gold has been greatly enhanced by these relatively recent developments. Several choices are available to investors interested in holding gold (or silver), which are discussed in more detail in the next section. Because it is much less widely traded than gold or silver, platinum still has a liquidity problem.

If you choose to hold gold or other precious metals in physical form, you will receive no interest or dividends. This is a significant drawback relative to alternate forms of investment that may yield substantial current return.

Gold Prices

Gold prices are established in three ways: by early trading in the Zurich interbank market, by the twice-daily London fixing by five merchant banks, and by the spot delivery contracts in the New York Commodity Exchange (Comex) and Chicago International Monetary Market.

Ways to Invest in Gold

There are several options for gold investment. But beware—not all are equally desirable.

Buying Bullion

For almost everyone in almost all circumstances, this is a bad idea. Don't buy bullion—for many reasons. You must take constructive delivery. You will have to bond and insure your holding. Because it is very cumbersome you will need a larger and larger safe-deposit box. Your investment will earn no interest or dividend. When you wish to sell it, no dealer will accept it without an assay or test of its purity—at your expense, of course.

In particular, avoid mail-order bullion buying. The companies that advertise mail-order sales say they will store the gold and give you depository receipts. Ostensibly, these warehouse receipts are negotiable instruments, and in the case of some reputable dealers they may be. Nonetheless, my advice is to stay out of long-distance mail-order gold because it is difficult to be certain that the gold you "own" actually exists.

Gold Coins

Coins are less cumbersome than bullion. If you have $100,000 in liquid assets, you might consider $10,000 in coins. The most popular ones, which are of very fine purity and uniform weight, have in the past been the Canadian maple leaf and the Mexican 50 peso. The American Stock Exchange makes a market for such coins through their American Gold Coin Exchange (ACGE). Interest in the Krugerrand is diminishing for political reasons, and minting of a U.S. gold coin is being considered.

Since 1980, the U.S. Treasury has minted one-ounce and half-ounce medallions honoring American creative artists. They are available through major banks and brokerage houses, which handle shipping, storage, and insurance through their depository or custodian banks. This investment method also avoids sales taxes, fabrication charges, and the need for assaying when the gold is sold.

A related investment are rare antique gold or silver coins, such as the St. Gauden $20 U.S. gold coin or the older $20 Liberty coin. These are as analogous to collectibles as to the investment-grade coins listed above. Thus, they require greater expertise of the investor—or a scrupulously honest dealer with a superb reputation. The condition of the coins greatly affects their market value, so a supposed "bargain" price may not be as great a bargain as it appears. Such coins, because their intrinsic value does not vary with taste or fashion, are more liquid than many other collectibles.

Commodity Futures

While precious metals are indeed commodities, I have already vehemently pointed out that commodities trading is for professionals and gamblers. Let me reiterate for emphasis: trading in *any* commodity is wrong for most investors and planners. If you choose to invest in precious metals, you are doing so as a means of diversifying your portfolio and *reducing* your overall risk.

Don't be seduced by the tremendous leveraging available to commodities traders; it cuts both ways. You make a lot of money one minute but lose it the next. That's what happens to at least 85 percent of commodities investors: they lose because they don't know what they're doing. Odds are that this probability applies to you.

Individual Mining-Company Stocks

A major advantage of gold-mining stocks over physical gold is that the stocks usually pay dividends to investors. The problem with these is that it is difficult to know which ones to choose. Canadian mining companies like Campbell Red Lake and American ones like Dome Mines and Homestake are all small, with limited trading volume and severe price fluctuations. They have relatively high production costs and low-grade ore.

International investing is fairly complicated. South African mines like Vaal Reefs or Doornfontein Gold Mining are ten times larger than the largest North American mines. These companies pay rather generous dividends. But South African law does not permit direct holdings by foreigners; you must purchase American Depository Receipts (ADRs).

ADRs are documents issued by an American bank in lieu of a stock certificate for shares in a foreign corporation; they are actively traded in the OTC market. They permit you to partake in any dividends, but are nonvoting. Americans currently hold almost a quarter of all South African gold shares. You will have to decide for yourself whether you are comfortable with the risk of political instability and the ethical questions inherent in South African investments.

Soviet mines, of course, do not issue stock; investment is unavailable to Americans.

Mutual Funds

Of all gold investments, I am most comfortable with mutual funds. They have greater liquidity if you want to get out, and they earn income for you (generally a 5- to 7-percent yield). But you must know what to look for: those well-managed mutual funds that have a diversified portfolio of gold-mining stocks and other forms of gold holdings from around the world and a proven track record in good years and bad years.

If you invest in a fund that goes up 200 percent in good years but gives back 150 percent in bad years, you lose. The mutual fund wins because they get their management fees in any case, plus commissions on any transaction. But you lose.

My criterion for a gold fund is the same as what I look for in any mutual fund: a little less gain in good years, but preservation of capital in bad years. If you choose your fund carefully and can take some risk, you can do well with such funds over a period of years. A few funds whose results you can check are the Oppenheimer Gold and Special Minerals Fund, Lexington Gold Fund, Goldconda Investors, Fidelity Precious Metals, and International Investors.

Silver

Silver is poor man's gold. It works pretty much the same as gold, but with some differences. One is that more silver is consumed annually than is produced from mines; the difference is made up by melting coins or jewelry and by industrial recycling. Silver is a strategic mineral that the Pentagon stockpiles for defense use.

If there are really massive international problems, gold is better because most foreign people are more comfortable with it. On the other hand, when our economy is going very well, I almost prefer silver because it has many industrial uses, such as in film manufacturing and electronic products.

Silver is traded on the same markets as gold, and silver-mining shares are also available. The price relationship between the two metals reflects the fact that both are subject to psychological factors such as fears of inflation. But silver's industrial uses mean its market price will follow its actual use value more closely.

Gemstones

Gems are not really suitable for the average investor, but they are fascinating to many people, so I am including a brief discussion of their investment characteristics and how they are appraised. Like precious metals, gemstones are a portable store of real wealth, as well as objects of aesthetic appeal. But the precious metals are unchanging elements, comparable in value for samples of equal size. Gems belong to the specialists, who alone can judge their relative quality.

As an investment, gems are characterized by unpredictable price fluctuations and lack of current cash return. Diamonds are more liquid than colored gemstones, but illiquidity is a disadvantage of all gemstones. Investors in gemstones are those who seek a hedge against political upheaval or precipitous declines in the value of paper money.

Diamonds as a commodity are almost totally controlled by DeBeers Consolidated Mines, Ltd., which sells an estimated $1.5 billion annually. About 20 percent of these are used for industrial purposes, and the overwhelming majority of the remainder for jewelry. Only the highest-quality gems, judged by both purity and whiteness, are considered investment stones. The Gemological Institute of America has set up a system for grading diamonds by color (D is the whitest) using a light box containing several pregraded stones. The diamonds are also graded for clarity. A flawless stone is one which has neither internal nor external flaws or inclusions under ten-power magnification. Finally, the other two "C"'s are cut and carat weight (a carat is one-fifth of a gram; there are 28 grams to the ounce). All these will be noted on the GIA certificate that accompanies any investment-grade diamond.

Colored stones are much more rare than diamonds. Since almost all such stones have inclusions, they are evaluated primarily by the depth and purity of their color. The range of color is also far greater than for diamonds, requiring greater expertise to judge these gems accurately. The quality of the light in which the stones are seen will also affect its appearance. In rubies, for example, those originating in Ceylon are pinkish, those from Thailand have a violet cast, and Burmese rubies are considered to have the purest red color. Many of these same countries are also the sites of sapphire mines, although the finest sapphires come from Kashmir in India. The finest emeralds, on the other hand, originate in one of four mines in the jungles of Colombia.

The geological pressures to which the stones are subjected during their formation and crystallization also produce characteristic inclusion patterns, the most common of which are called rutile needles, by which the trained eye can distinguish their origin. The nature and type of these inclusions can also indicate whether or not the gem is genuine.

Experts recommend placing a small fraction of one's assets in a balanced portfolio of four gems: a one-carat Burmese or two-carat Thai ruby, a one-carat Kashmir or two-carat Burmese sapphire, a one- to two-carat Colombia emerald, and a one-carat D-flawless diamond. At this time, such a portfolio would represent an investment of $80,000 to $100,000, so this is really an investment strategy for the wealthy. Those among us of more average income should probably enjoy a very occasional purchase of gem jewelry and leave investment gems to the rich.

Conclusion

If you believe that inflation will continue or accelerate in years to come because of national debt, that international turmoil will persist, that the dollar is overvalued and will seek a lower level, consider gold. At $320–$330 a troy ounce, it could be near its low. In my opinion, the downside risk of gold today is no more than 5–10 percent, whereas its upside potential, if any of these problems do come about, is unlimited. Gold as a safety hedge, an insurance policy, to offset major unforeseeable price movements in liquid assets, makes good sense. Other metals and gemstones do not offer the relative liquidity and marketability of gold.

Do a pro forma, and if your other needs are adequately covered, you may decide to put 5 to 15 percent of your assets in gold for long-term appreciation and insurance.

PART III

PROTECTING YOUR ASSETS

CHAPTER 12

FINE ART
AND COLLECTIBLES

Remember your enthusiastic childhood preoccupation with your collection of baseball cards, your HO gauge Lionel trains, your Beatles albums? Do you smile at your kid's collection of Madonna posters or E.T. memorabilia? Laugh no more; these items could become (or may already be) investment-grade entertainment collectibles.

Investment-grade collectibles are tangible objects that have historic significance within the culture of their time and place because of their use of current technology and their reflection of the popular amusements of the day. They should be relatively scarce and in excellent condition. Their special attributes include their perishability, continuing production as a genre, mass-market appeal, and timeliness as a reflection of the culture that produced them.

Fine Art

The simple dictionary definition is "the conscious use of skill, taste, and creative imagination in the production of aesthetic objects." Limited-edition reproductions can be included if they are produced by the artist (or under his or her direct supervision) and are limited to reasonable numbers.

Valuing particular works, short of putting the items up for auction to see what they will bring, is always difficult. However, independent appraisals by two or more reputable dealers (not including the one who is selling you the object) can often help set a range.

The fine-art market has four main participants: private collectors or investors, dealers and auctioneers, institutions or museums, and, of course, the artists themselves. Each has its own function in the market.

Judging Quality

The value of a work of art is based on four characteristics: its condition, rarity, quality with respect to the skill of execution, and historic importance. (A related criterion is provenance, or history of ownership.) Within the works of a particular artist or craftsman, the price of a particular piece will depend additionally on the desirability of that period in the artist's career, the quantity of his works and their availability in the private market, the presence or absence of a signature, and the item's size and subject.

Investing vs. Collecting

If one applies the criteria of aesthetic worth, originality, and authenticity very stringently, one is a legitimate investor. Collectors also focus on a particular specialty, but apply fewer criteria. Accumulators are more eclectic and casual in their approach.

Fine art and more traditional investment-grade collectibles like furniture, rugs, or books depend in part for their value on their aesthetic appeal. The degree of aesthetic significance assigned to the work of a particular individual or period, however, is greatly affected by the popular taste of the moment among the cognescenti. The most effective investor in fine art will combine impeccable taste and timing with financial acumen.

Appropriate Investing in Fine Art and Collectibles

Like precious metals or gemstones, these categories of tangibles are most appropriate for those who have much of their financial portfolio already in place. In such a portfolio, tangibles provide a store of value complementary to that represented by other investments.

Works of art and collectibles are assets with intrinsic value. One's tangible assets can add appreciably to one's net worth. Of course, these objects can provide a great deal of enjoyment, and many of them also have use value. But they must be well-managed to guard against security and environmental hazards if they are to bring pleasure to your children, too.

Although one can certainly make money in antique toys or Oriental rugs when the time is ripe and they are riding the crest of fashion, price appreciation is chancy—and reversible. Unlike traditional investments, the market for these collectibles is not standardized; nor are the items themselves available for trading on a regular basis. *Therefore, the most important criterion for collectibles is your interest in and love for the genre you choose.* Plan to hold your collectibles for a long period, at least five years.

Entertainment-oriented Collectibles

An authoritative source on entertainment-related collectibles names eight categories for which there are active markets and which may, therefore, have legitimate investment potential:

Toys—the highest prices at auction, often over $1,000, are fetched by those in top condition. Collectors often specialize in dolls, cast-iron toys, trains, or robots.

Movie memorabilia—from props to press kits. The greatest recent appreciation, as one might expect, has been in Reagan material.

Comic books—the rarest, Marvel Comics No. 1, has sold for well over $10,000.

Baseball cards—a passion since their introduction in the 1860s, with many cards now bringing over $1,000 at auction.

Advertisements—from the 1850s onward, they illustrate technological advances in color printing and lithography.

Games—board games in their original boxes are most valuable.

Posters—more accessible than fine art, prized both for their graphic design and their historic context.

So-called "fantasy art," usually created between 1890 and 1937 by artists such as Aubrey Beardsley, and showing creatures that don't exist in real life, like gremlins or unicorns.

Avoid rip-offs in these or any other collectible field by finding a dealer of scrupulous integrity, excellent reputation, and demonstrated expertise. The finest of the major dealers or market masters, if they so choose, can provide invaluable education. Learn as much as you can. You are best protected by becoming a bit of an expert yourself. This means, for example, becoming able to judge accurately, or "grade," the physical condition of collectibles: from poor through mint.

Indeed, this is part of the fun of investment collectibles—and you should be having fun! (Otherwise, you may as well be grimly reading the options tables.) Since these entertainment collectibles do not yet have the popularity and recognition of postage stamps or Oriental rugs, they are more affordable, with fewer knowledgeable investors competing. And they have tremendous growth potential.

Coins and Stamps

These are by far the most popular collectibles. They are both widely known and widely available, with extensive markets for active traders. You may consider your coin or stamp collection as a hobby, or pursue it more seriously as an investor. The nature of your interest and the depth of your purse will determine the quality and rarity of the coins or stamps you seek for your collection.

Risks of Investing

Investing in collectibles is not without risk. Two of the greatest risks are the volatility of popular taste as it affects market values, and the misrepresentation of quality by ignorant or unscrupulous dealers. Outright fakes can be a problem with collectibles such as fine period furniture.

Another possibility with some types of collectibles is what is called a "warehouse find," a large previously unknown cache that can be dumped on the marketplace and lower the value of that type of collectible drastically. (More sophisticated dealers will dispose of such a find discreetly to prime collectors, or gradually to the open market in a manner analogous to the way DeBeers controls the availability of diamonds.)

Buying Guidelines

Perhaps the most important single admonition is to buy what you like. Assume that you will live with it rather than sell it or donate it. Within your budget, buy the best available. If the quality is questionable, wait for something better.

While long-term relative market values are relatively constant, there are large short-term fluctuations. Entertainment collectibles within a particular category, for example, usually have related three- to eight-year market cycles. This information can be used to your advantage if you are investing for appreciation as well as for enjoyment. Essentially, these cycles can enable you to buy wholesale when demand is at low ebb and sell retail near the peak of demand, rather than the other way around.

Another way to accomplish a similar objective, once you have become relatively knowledgeable, is to buy from fellow collectors. Dealers pay only half the retail for what they buy. A collector will usually sell to a peer at 75 percent of retail, to the advantage of both parties.

To learn the market for your collectibles, consult specialty periodicals, collectors' magazines, and auction catalogues. Visit antique shops and attend flea markets (talking to as many dealers as possible), estate sales, auctions, and collectors' conventions (prices will be a bit higher, but the quality and quantity of merchandise will often more than compensate). Examine with appropriate caution the most authoritative price guides in your field of choice.

Don't forget that once you own a collection, you will have the usual headaches of insurance and custodial care, compounded by the intrinsic fragility of these items that may require special preservation techniques and protection against environmental hazards. Do what you must for optimum protection.

CHAPTER 13

SHELTERING YOUR INCOME FROM TAXES

Those fortunate enough to acquire substantial amounts of money find themselves with a new problem: how to keep as much of it as possible, while sending as little as possible to the IRS. They must search diligently for tax shelters. If you are lucky enough to have reached the upper marginal brackets but haven't yet determined how best to protect your income from the IRS, read on. (Those who have not yet reached the 50-percent bracket, but expect increases in income, will also find valuable ideas for planning in this chapter.)

What Is a Tax Shelter?

Here is how I define the term: A tax shelter offers an opportunity to turn part of your tax bill into profitable assets. It is an investment that is structured to produce enough deductions or write-offs to offset the income from the investment itself, plus some left over to offset income from other sources.

It does this by using three major categories of tax benefit: deductions sheltering current income from other sources, deductions offsetting future income from investments, and use of contributions and deductions to purchase assets, which, if profitable, will be taxed at lower long-term capital gain rates when sold. Because each of these benefits is somewhat at odds with the others, there is no ideal shelter that maximizes all three. You must choose a tax shelter whose emphasis best suits your needs.

Many kinds of investments are *tax-advantaged*. By far the most commonly used is the home-mortgage interest deduction. Probably the second most common device for tax reduction is long-term gain on securities transactions, now taxed at a top rate of 20 percent (whereas the top rate for earned income is currently 50 percent). Also on the list are familiar investments like municipal bonds and newer products like universal life insurance that are also exempt from taxation. Series E U.S. Savings Bonds, IRAs, Keoghs, and deferred annuities are *tax-deferred* until maturity or retirement age. But none is a true tax shelter.

Someone making $60,000 earned income plus another $15,000 in interest and dividends has obviously moved into a relatively high bracket. Such an individual should use tax-advantaged investments like those listed above to defer some income or gains, and thus defer taxes. On the other hand, someone making $150,000 in earned income plus $25,000 worth of interest and dividends is in the top marginal tax bracket and should be considering true tax shelters.

What Are Tax Shelters Used For?

Sheltering Current Income

Probably the commonest use is to reduce taxes on high-level recurring income. Deep shelters are designed for the investor whose primary concern is immediate and continuing relief from his tax burden, rather than income or capital gains.

Let's look at how a properly chosen shelter can generate write-offs for this individual. We assume a 42-percent tax bracket, $15,000 invested, and a shelter with a 100-percent first-year write-off (using 1984 tax-rate schedules for a married taxpayer filing jointly).

	No Shelter	With Tax Shelter
Adjusted gross income	$75,000	$75,000
Shelter investment		15,000
Shelter deduction		(15,000)
Revised taxable income	75,000	60,000
Tax due	21,468	15,168
First-year tax savings		$ 6,300

Building Assets

Equity builders are for people who wish to build assets as well as shelter income from taxes. Investing in this kind of shelter during peak earning years can help you strengthen your total asset base before you retire. These tax shelters will probably protect only current cash flow, but should have good promise of strong capital appreciation. You may also wish to reinvest shelter income to pyramid your deductions while you increase your overall assets.

Limitations on the Use of Tax Shelters

Recapture

Tax shelters once were often used to reduce the tax burden from other long-term capital gains. But this is not as common since recent tax bills restricted one's ability to report profit as a long-term gain. The IRS may adjust your basis (or original cost) in an asset to reflect depreciation or depletion deductions already claimed. By reducing your basis, your gain is larger and the capital-gains tax higher.

Worse, a portion of the profit may now be subject to "recapture" of deductions at ordinary rates. Recapture is merely a way of letting the IRS get you the second time around if they miss you the first time. When a tax-shelter partnership sells assets for a profit, the IRS may disallow your share of the profits as capital gains, treating them instead as recaptured deductions from earlier in the shelter program. In that case, the gain is taxed at ordinary rates of up to 50 percent, rather than the maximum 20-percent long-term gains rate.

Alternative Minimum Tax

This is another unpleasant and complicated aside, but one which may be important to you and your advisers in determining whether a particular shelter is an appropriate investment for you.

Certain "tax preference" items are taxable at a 15-percent rate after the first $10,000. This is known as the minimum tax. Of the nine tax preferences, four relate to tax shelters: the accelerated portion of any real property depreciation, the accelerated portion of depreciation of leased personal property, the portion of depletion that exceeds your adjusted cost basis in an oil well (see oil and gas investments, p. 158), and the intangible drilling costs on successful well completions that exceed straight-line cost recovery.

The 1978 Tax Law created an "alternative minimum tax" that you must pay if the amount exceeds your regular income tax and the minimum tax combined. Its purpose is to keep high-income taxpayers from sheltering all their income and paying no taxes. It prevents the kind of free and easy use of shelters that prevailed before by making the practice far less lucrative.

The tax is assessed at a rate of 10 percent on amounts of $20,000 to $60,000 and 20 percent on amounts over

$60,000. The tax base is the sum of: (1) taxable income, (2) excess itemized deductions (those over 60 percent of adjusted gross income), and (3) the untaxed portion of capital gains. High-income taxpayers should be aware of the alternative minimum tax in planning their investments.

Overinvesting

Once some people discover tax shelters and learn how effective they can be, they get too enthusiastic. Make sure that you are not sheltering so much that your taxable income is lowered to a bracket in which sheltering is no longer desirable. One simple way to do this is by performing analysis: (1) figure out the amount of available cash you have for investments, (2) determine the minimum amount of taxable income that is desirable for you, and (3) calculate the dollar amount of tax savings or the number of brackets you could reduce by using your available cash to purchase shelters.

Limited Partnerships

Most tax shelters are *limited partnerships.* A limited partnership is simply an organizational *format* for investment, like a mutual fund or an option. The structure of a limited partnership is extremely flexible and can be used to serve many objectives, not only those of tax shelters. Its chief characteristic as it relates to tax shelters is that the deductions and income of the partnership are not taxed to the partnership itself, but pass through proportionally to the individual returns of the partners.

There are two parties to the agreement: the *general partner,* who claims expertise in a certain field of business like real estate or oil and gas, manages the business of the partnership, and makes all operating decisions; and the *limited partners,* who need not be knowledgeable about the business. Their role is simply to provide the capital to finance the program, and to participate in any gains or losses.

The "limits" on the limited partners are two: (1) they have no say in the management of the partnership, and (2) their liability is limited to the amounts of their respective investments in the partnership.

Disadvantages

Other characteristics of most limited partnerships are relatively high risk and illiquidity. If the program or deal proposed in the prospectus turns out to be unprofitable, the general partner will collect its management fees anyhow. But the limited partners stand to lose some (or all) of their initial investments. Besides this investment risk, there is tax risk. We've all seen how frequently and drastically Congress can change the tax laws, sometimes retroactively. Judicial interpretation can also adversely affect previously legitimate deductions.

With the exception of some real estate syndication shares from the boom of the past several years, there is often no secondary market in partnership units. Some general partners will agree to repurchase shares from limited partners after two years or more, under conditions that are almost invariably disadvantageous to the limited partner. The reality is that investment in a limited partnership generally requires a *long-term* commitment, perhaps five to seven years or more.

Public vs. Private Offerings

Tax shelters are offered to investors in two ways. Public shelters are required to register with the SEC and make full disclosure to investors through their offering prospectuses.

The marketing agents for these partnerships, usually brokerage firms, also exercise "due diligence," the application of informed judgment designed to determine the competence of the general partners.

Generally, public offerings collect smaller sums of money from far greater numbers of investors than private offerings. The minimum investment can be as little as $5,000. Usually, the prospective investor is required to show a net worth of $30,000 (exclusive of primary residence and automobiles) and a $30,000 annual income, or a net worth of $75,000. Higher requirements exist in some states.

Because their capital pool is larger, public partnerships are able to diversify more, using the limited partners' funds to purchase, for example, several income properties or several oil wells at different locations.

Private offerings, on the other hand, are usually made available only to investors of very substantial means: net worth of $1 million or annual income over $200,000. The investor must show himself to be "accredited" by previous purchases, or have great investment sophistication.

Minimum purchases may be $35,000, $50,000, or even more. Private placements usually involve the purchase of a single property, so they lack the diversification of most public offerings. Advantages are that expenses are lower because SEC registration is not required, and payments or contributions can be staged over several years, which increases tax savings.

Criteria for Choosing Tax-sheltered Investments

With tax shelters, as with any other investment, what is appropriate for you will depend on your personal situation and your tolerance for risk. If tax benefit is your primary motive, you will want a deep shelter, but you may still choose between subsidized housing and shelter-oriented real estate leasing deals. Equity builders include conventionally financed real estate, oil and gas drilling partnerships, and timber. Any of these would be undertaken more in the expectation of profit than for tax benefits per se; they differ primarily in the degree of risk.

Risk Tolerance

There are different levels of *risk vs. rewards*. You can go into an ultraconservative limited partnership that has very little leverage. The general partner takes the investors' contributions and uses them pretty much as the total amount of the capitalization. This is done most often in real estate partnerships, but can also be in oil and gas, R & D, or even equipment leasing. It's all in the way it's structured. Each one, no matter which field it's in, can be structured to be ultraconservative, middle-of-the-road, or very aggressive.

Basically, you have to ask yourself on a risk scale of 1 to 10 how conservative or aggressive you are.

For example, in real estate you can buy an ultraconservative, very balanced program for your $10,000 investment. You get nominal write-offs, probably about 80–85 percent in tax write-offs over the first three or four years. If you're in a 40-percent bracket, you'll save $4,000 in hard cash immediately—taxes you won't have to pay. So you've really only got $6,000 at risk, which will generate additional write-offs and, later, cash flow. It is hoped that by the end of a five- or seven-year program, when the property is sold and the gains distributed, the sum of your cash flow and capital gains should be anywhere from two to three times your original contribution, *unrelated to any tax benefit*. That is a reasonably successful, balanced real estate program.

That's the type of program, with a proven track record, that we like to see in a general partner, and we have confidence in recommending such people to our clients. They make their money, you make your money, and you have a good, solid investment. Go with the track record of the general partner on proven results.

Management Quality

Examine the reputation and track record of the general partner: what are the proven results of his previous partnerships? You probably can't obtain this information easily. You should contact someone knowledgeable, someone you trust.

Have an adviser look at it who understands how tax shelters are put together. He can tell you how it's leveraged, how it's financed, what the fees are, what the commissions are, and all the other things you don't want to be concerned about. If you are a client of a major brokerage firm, it should have first-rate due diligence procedures that will eliminate from consideration over 90 percent of all limited partnership tax shelters. If your broker can't offer this service, find one who can. (If you have any difficulty with this, write to me or call, and I'll be happy to provide the names of people in your geographic area who can assist you.)

Assessability

This refers to the right of the general partner to return to the limited partners for additional capital infusions after the initial payment. Generally, avoid shelters with even partial assessability. If the deal looks terrific otherwise, go ahead. But be prepared for additional assessments.

Be wary of tax shelters with high write-offs issued at the end of the year. Some of these programs get put together hastily and the benefits diminish. And finally, be sure the general partner's fees for the deal are not out of line with industry standards for similar programs.

Types of Tax-sheltered Investments

Real Estate

The population of the United States is likely to continue growing, whereas the supply of available land will not. For these reasons, if interest rates remain stable, real estate will continue to be very sound. On the other hand, if interest rates go up or the tax preferences for real estate are reduced significantly, then real estate will be knocked out of the box.

Today 70–75 percent of tax shelters involve *real estate*. One reason for this is the comparative advantage real estate has in the tax laws vis-à-vis other forms of shelter. The laws now prohibit individual investors from deducting losses from a business activity in excess of the amount they have at risk (the cash investment and adjusted basis, plus any personal liability). These "at risk" rules apply to all tax shelters except real estate, meaning you need not assume personal liability for any part of the partnership's mortgages on the buildings and land in the program in order to claim deductions. Depreciation schedules of only 15 years for real property, established by the 1981 tax act, also enhanced the popularity of real estate investments.

Most real estate programs invest in one of five areas: existing improved real estate, new improved real estate, government-assisted housing, raw land, and rehabilitated buildings. Rehabilitation projects have become particularly attractive since the 15-year depreciation provisions and investment tax credits of up to 25 percent became available.

Raw land is generally a bad idea because it generates no income or write-offs until it is developed. Government-assisted housing used to be a very good shelter with high write-offs, but cuts in federal housing programs during the Reagan administration have made this form of tax shelter almost extinct.

The sponsor may define the properties in advance or may retain flexibility by investing in an unspecified "blind pool" of properties, to be selected later in accordance with objectives spelled out in the prospectus.

The two greatest risks in real estate investment are poor location and poor management. Investing in a blind pool limits your ability to judge the suitability of location, thus placing even greater reliance on the management capability of the general partner.

For people who can afford to invest $20,000 to $30,000, there are many attractive real estate investments. The two main types of partnerships are:

Leveraged Programs

In high-leveraged programs, most of the purchase price of the partnership's properties is borne by lenders. Deductions are based on debt service for the mortgages, plus depreciation. These are deep-shelter deals for high-bracket households.

These programs frequently invest in new improved real estate, building on raw land, or purchasing newly constructed properties. These generate deductions through leverage, fees, interest, and depreciation. They attempt to recover the limited partners' investment through tax savings in five to seven years. But greater risk is entailed with new properties, because it is hard to predict how quickly they will be leased or sold.

In examining the prospectus, note whether the sponsors will invest in residential or nonresidential property and what depreciation method is proposed. If the partnership elects accelerated rather than straight-line depreciation, the *full amount* depreciated on nonresidential property will be subject to recapture at ordinary income rates, whereas on residential property only the *difference* between accelerated and straight-line depreciation is subject to recapture.

More conservative programs

These programs use little or no borrowing or leveraging. They are designed for safety. They may invest in existing improved properties where the cash flow is faster and more predictable. They generate moderate deductions and moderate capital-gains possibilities with lower risk than new properties.

They are good for people in lower tax brackets, such as retirees, who are looking for maximum income. Some of these are insured as to income. In addition, they can be a viable hedge against inflation.

One extremely safe and very appealing variation of this type of real estate partnership is one that purchases and leases commercial property on a *triple-net lease* basis. "Triple net" means that the tenant, not the lessor, is responsible for taxes, insurance, and maintenance. These partnerships look for high-quality firms with top-notch credit ratings that are planning to build a corporate headquarters, a retail store, or a franchise outlet.

Oil and Gas

While gas and oil prices have declined recently, and OPEC seems to be on the defensive, many knowledgeable people feel these setbacks are temporary and believe the long-term future of the industry remains bright. How you feel is a matter of individual research and judgment. If you decide oil and gas are for you, you can invest in a tax-sheltered partnership.

The two kinds of oil and gas investments are exploratory

and development programs. Exploratory programs are commonly known as "wildcats," wells drilled in areas where there has been no established production. Their odds of success are about one in ten. Development wells, on the other hand, are drilled in areas of previous discoveries. They have a success rate of 60 to 70 percent, but your general partner can still drill a "dry hole." If you get lucky with a wildcatter, you stand to make a high level of gain for your risk. But the payoff will be slower than in a development program, for three reasons: the need to drill deeper, the extra time and money to gear up for production in a new area, and the need to pay off the lenders before cash flow starts going to investors.

Oil and gas are still tax-favored, although that may change in the latest 1985–86 round of tax reform. Currently, in addition to generous first-year deductions, these programs can usually shelter up to one-half of later income from producing wells through the depletion allowance. Depletion recognizes the finite nature of mineral deposits by treating them as wasting assets, and providing a special deduction intended to encourage investment in exploration.

Equipment Leasing

This has become an increasingly popular method of financing capital assets like rolling stock, airplanes, ships, machinery, and even computers. ERTA made very attractive rule changes that allow for quicker depreciation and lower taxation of cash distributions. Also, tax credits are available to investors in the riskier operating-equipment leasing transactions, in which investors purchase the asset and hire a manager to find an industrial user.

Most equipment leasing programs borrow 75 to 90 percent of the cost of the equipment from lending institutions and seek the remainder from limited partners.

The primary tax benefit of equipment leasing is tax *deferral*. You invest during a high-liability time and deduct a large amount of depreciation, front-end expenses, borrowing costs, and investment tax credit in the early years.

The sponsor or general partner is usually an equipment broker, who may be with a large national concern or a small local one. The manager's compensation is derived from initial fees, management fees, and a share of the residual value of the equipment after the lease expires. As always, the skill and expertise of this general partner are critical to the success of the program.

"Exotic" Tax Shelters

These include agricultural programs like cattle breeding (or raising) and timber; cable television and film production; alternative energy like ethanol; and research and development (R & D). The nature of the tax and economic benefits derived may vary among these types of shelters. For example, cable TV partnerships aim at capital appreciation with investment tax credits and high deductions. R & D partnerships provide shelter for capital contributions and, if successful, royalties that are taxed as long-term capital gains.

Be very careful of the amount of write-offs offered to you. Again, buy for the economics. Look for cash flow and long-term capital gains as well as write-offs. You should be in a relatively high tax bracket and keep track of frequent changes in the legislation that may reduce the desirability of some shelters while enhancing others.

Abusive Shelters

What you don't want is to get involved in so-called *abusive tax shelters*. You should not risk a single dollar of your investment funds in this type of program. Abusive tax shelters have no basic economic justification; they are set up solely to generate inflated write-offs that can be charged against your other earnings. They are illegal and dishonest, and the company that markets them may well go out of business.

Sometimes even worse horror stories can happen. I was involved in a particularly awful case recently in which I was quite helpless to prevent the inevitable. Several years ago an aggressive self-employed businessman invested $45,000 in a coal-mining tax shelter. His financial adviser told him not to do it. His brother-in-law, a CPA and full partner in one of the Big Eight accounting firms, told him not to do it. He did it anyway. The following year he died.

The widow came in to see us a few years later when the IRS disallowed the whole shelter, but of course by that time there was very little we could do for her. She had to repay it all: the original investment plus interest and huge penalties. For several intervening years she was penalized 20 percent. The penalties and interest charges totaled more than twice the original amount, for a sum of about $140,000. To add insult to injury, for each day of delay she was obligated to pay another 12- to 15-percent annual interest and late fees. The IRS took every dime.

I have no doubt that couple should have had some money invested in tax shelters. But they didn't act prudently and do their homework—or listen to the people who did it for them—and she was punished harshly for her husband's improvidence.

This is the difference between tax *avoidance* and tax *evasion*. Tax avoidance is legal and you can do it with qualified tax shelters. Tax evasion is basically illegal abuse of tax shelters.

Often, abusive shelters will be disallowed by the IRS and penalties charged the investors. As we have seen, once that decision has been made, the burden is on the taxpayer to pay immediately, no matter how astronomical the charges.

I cannot overemphasize the importance of examining the sponsor's integrity and history, and the economics of the deal. If they don't make sense *exclusive* of the tax benefits, don't buy. If competent professional advisers strongly oppose the purchase, heed them. Reckless disregard of expert advice in these instances can cost you more money. For your own peace of mind, as well as for the safety of your money, don't ever get involved in an abusive shelter.

Tax shelter summary

Know they're available. Know you can go into public or private shelters. Always look for equity buildup. Examine the track record of the general partner. Most important, buy for economic justification, not tax avoidance alone. Avoid abusive shelters at all costs. Follow the advice of someone you trust. If you buy the wrong shelter, you'll wish you had given the money to your favorite charity. At least you would get a tax break the IRS is unlikely to question.

CHAPTER 14

PREPARING FOR RETIREMENT

This is one of the most enduring and serious tasks for any mature individual. With today's demographics, those of us now in the prime earning years cannot take for granted that Social Security benefits will be available or adequate to sustain us in comfort when we reach age 65. Nor, with increasing longevity, can we be blithely certain that our life savings will last as long as our lives do.

Congress has given us the strongest possible clues to its judgment that Social Security, in the years ahead, may become an even less adequate source of retirement income. It has enacted a series of laws designed to enhance the appeal of retirement-oriented investments. And Americans have responded with enthusiasm to some plans, such as IRAs, though not to others.

What all this means is that we must all begin to think in terms of *self-reliance and self-insurance.* We need to provide for our own increasingly long and likely retirement years. This chapter will discuss the many tools now available to meet this need.

As in any other type of savings plan for whatever purpose, the primary lesson is to pay yourself first. If you don't take at least 10 percent of your earned income right off the top, before you pay your bills or indulge in whatever kinds of discretionary spending you enjoy, you are likely to come to your retirement years with nothing. Imagine yourself as a ward of the state, or dependent on the charity of your children. That should motivate you to set aside a reasonable amount every payday toward your retirement. You don't have to do it all yourself. Let Uncle Sam and your employer help you. But if you want your retirement to be financially comfortable and secure, you must bear much of the responsibility.

One reason this is so critically important is that inflation rates are unpredictable and most employer plans are not inflation-adjusted. Similarly, most annuities have a fixed payoff amount. Social Security cost-of-living adjustments were unduly generous for some years, but they have already been scaled back and are likely to be cut further in the growing concern over the deficit. Therefore, it is especially important that you invest your portion of your retirement nest egg with an eye toward capital appreciation or relatively high income. This will prepare you to face future inflation without undue concern.

Another reason to become more self-reliant in your retirement planning is that a postretirement reduction in living standards is no longer generally accepted. Most people today reach retirement age in better health, and they want to have the financial capacity to travel and pursue other interests as long as health permits. You will probably feel this way, too. So you need to plan for a postretirement life that won't cramp your style.

Social Security

Although this was never the congressional intent, many Americans continue to rely on Social Security to provide most, if not all, of their income when they retire. (An estimated one-quarter of the 18 million retirees receiving benefits have no other income.) Once a worker becomes eligible by amassing forty quarters (ten years) of covered employment, including six of the thirteen quarters preceding retirement, he or she is entitled to benefits beginning at age sixty-five, or at a lower rate if she or he chooses to retire before the ages of sixty-two and sixty-five. The benefit amount is determined by a formula based on covered earnings during one's working years, so it will vary by income. The spouse of a covered worker is entitled to 50 percent of his or her benefit, and dependent children under age eighteen to a child's benefit of 50 percent, with a maximum monthly family limit. In addition, Social Security provides disability benefits, survivor benefits, and health insurance benefits (through Medicare).

While it would be foolish to rely on Social Security exclusively for one's retirement income, it is equally foolish to ignore it in planning for retirement. You should check once every few years with your Social Security branch office to determine the size of your account and the number of quarters of credit you have. One reason for doing so is to check the accuracy of the Social Security Administration's records; the agency is *not* required to correct errors unless you report them within three years. Certain errors could adversely affect your benefits.

Once assured that you are eligible for coverage, make your best estimate of average annual income for the duration of your career until retirement. Then use this rule of thumb to estimate your benefits: middle-income earners (around $17,000 a year) will receive Social Security payments averaging 42 percent of salary; low-wage earners 55 percent; and higher-income people ($35,000 and up) about 28 percent of the Social Security wage base.

Both husband and wife should do this analysis, and the spouse with the lesser earnings should claim benefits in his or her own name *or* plan on using the higher earner's benefit (50 percent). The lower-earning worker is entitled to the higher of the two benefits, but not to both.

The available retirement plans depend in part on the nature of your work: whether you are a corporate employee, self-employed, a member of a professional corporation, or the head of your own business. While employee-related retirement options can be quite complex, not all will apply to any given individual's situation. Let's review the main ones.

Private Pension Funds

Vesting

This key concept refers to the employee's right to benefits based on the employer's contribution, and not subject to the employee's continuing to work for the same employer. Your employer's plan may provide for immediate vesting (the most liberal and least likely), partial vesting on a percentage basis over several years, or full vesting only after a waiting period of five years or more.

Contributory vs. noncontributory

In a noncontributory plan, only the employer pays into the retirement fund. A contributory plan is one to which the employee also makes payments. You are always entitled to a refund of your own contribution to a plan, usually with interest, even if you leave the company before your benefits have fully vested.

Retirement age

Most plans establish a normal retirement age, usually sixty-five, and often a minimum-service requirement as well. Some may provide for early retirement at reduced benefit levels, or for disability retirement. Some may also set a mandatory retirement age, often seventy.

If you and others work on a sustained basis for a company, the company probably has a *formal pension plan,* which describes your rights and eligibility standards, and the formula for calculating the amount of benefits to which you are entitled.

A *qualified* plan goes further by meeting standards set forth in the 1974 Employee Retirement Income Security Act (ERISA). It requires that the plan be a legally binding agreement for the exclusive benefit of the employees or their beneficiaries, that its principal and income be impossible to divert and use for any other purpose, and that the plan benefit a broad class of employees rather than discriminating in favor of officers or executives.

Tax advantages
Such a plan has several tax advantages:

Its benefits are not taxed as income until distributed.

Earnings on investments made with contributed funds are also not taxed until paid out.

The employer's contributions are deductible as business expense.

Death benefits attributable to employer contributions and paid in installments to a named beneficiary are not taxable to the employee's gross estate.

A lump-sum distribution upon severance of employment may be taxed on a favorable basis (see the discussion of lump-sum distributions later in this chapter).

The magic of compound interest
When you defer income taxes by making regular contributions to an IRA the equity build-up over time is astonish-

ing. Because the amounts invested and the annual earnings are not taxed until they are withdrawn, a substantially larger sum is at work earning interest for you.

Benefits

In addition to the retirement pension around which qualified plans are built, other benefits are usually available to vested employees. These include:

Disability payments for certain employees (usually early retirement for long-term employees at reduced benefit levels).

Medical expense benefits for retired employees.

A pension and/or a lump-sum death benefit payable to a surviving spouse in the event of the participant's death before retirement or after retirement if the benefits paid by that time have not exceeded the amount he contributed to the plan.

Benefits payable from *employer* contributions upon termination of employment. (An employee is always entitled, as a minimum, to the return of his own contributions.) The *benefit amount* will depend largely on the formula elected by the employer. *Defined-contribution* or "money-purchase" formulas set aside a percentage of the employee's pay, and use the proceeds to purchase a retirement benefit when needed.

Defined-benefit formulas may be related to years of service only (flat amount-unit benefit or percentage-unit benefit formula), to earnings only (flat-percentage formula), or to neither (flat-amount formula). Usually these formulas use the final average salary, or the earnings during the employee's highest compensation years, to determine benefit amounts, rather than using a career average that takes into account workers' lower earnings earlier in their careers. The vested benefits of employees in companies with this sort of qualified plan are insured by the Pension Benefit Guaranty Corporation, even if the company goes out of business.

Some plans, called integrated plans, consider Social Security benefits in determining the pension amount to which the employee is entitled. Generally, integrated pension plans reduce the benefit amount by a percentage of the Social Security benefit, or provide a lower benefit on the proportion of wages subject to Social Security.

ERISA also sets maximum-benefit limits for annual payments under qualified plans: either 100 percent of average annual compensation for the three highest consecutive earning years or $90,000 (subject to annual cost-of-living adjustments), whichever is less. The totals are reduced proportionally for employees with fewer than ten years of service. These will be of interest only to high-income employees.

Pension benefits and inflation

The vulnerability of your benefits to purchasing-power risk, or inflation, is a matter for grave concern. Several adjustment techniques are available to lessen the negative impact. Most effective, of course, is a cost-of-living plan that adjusts for Consumer Price Index variations. Another is the variable annuity, which invests pension contributions in a portfolio of equity securities and purchases a lifetime retirement income with the proceeds. Ostensibly, these protect against inflation, but at the risk of loss of capital. Finally, retirement plans that base their benefits on final salary take recent inflation into account better than career-earnings plans. If your employer has no inflation adjustment policies, you will need to plan even more carefully to meet this burden yourself.

Profit-sharing Plans

These are similar in objectives to pension plans, but they relate employer contributions to profits rather than to payroll. As a by-product, they often offer generous severance benefits. Most contributory plans offer withdrawal and loan privileges. If these are available to you, remember that loans are preferred because the borrowed funds are not treated as taxable income.

Whatever plan your employer offers, and however complex it may seem to you, take any steps necessary to familiarize yourself with its provisions. Ask the personnel department to answer all the questions you have, but make sure you understand what you and your family are entitled to, and whether any actions you might take could jeopardize those benefits. If the plan is not integrated with Social Security, make your own best estimates for determining how much you need to set aside for your own retirement.

401K Plans

401K is a new and increasingly popular tax-preferred retirement plan. It permits employees to reduce their taxable income by putting up to 15 percent of pretax salary and bonuses (up to $30,000 a year) in a qualified savings plan, with taxes deferred until the money is distributed. The money can be withdrawn without penalty before retirement for "financial hardship," which includes disability, or if the employee leaves the company. Ten-year forward averaging can be used to reduce the tax liability on such a distribution. One may also contribute to a personal IRA. Not surprisingly, 401K has been met with enthusiasm by employees, but it's an administrative headache for employers. They are required to show that the levels of contribution by the top one-third and bottom two-thirds of employees are within antidiscrimination guidelines. Record-keeping problems associated with this requirement have slowed the acceptance of 401K plans. Pending tax-law changes may reduce the benefit.

Tax-sheltered Annuity Plans

These arrangements permit employees of qualified organizations to set aside part of their pretax earnings for retirement. Eligible organizations include public and private schools and colleges, tax-exempt charitable and scientific organizations like the Salvation Army or the Sierra Club, and nonprofit hospitals. IRAs are very advantageous and flexible for those who are qualified.

A special feature of this type of annuity is the privilege to roll over an existing annuity for another paying higher returns: the so-called 1035 tax-free exchange or rollover, usually without penalty or tax consequences.

Retirement Planning for the Self-employed

Under HR-10 or the Keogh Act of 1962 (as amended), sole proprietorships and partnerships can have qualified pension and profit-sharing plans with tax benefits similar to those for other employers. That is, plan contributions are fully deductible to the self-employed person and other participants, and the contributions also accumulate tax-free.

Since 1982, these benefits have become more generous. Self-employed individuals may now contribute 25 percent of earned income, up to $30,000 per year. However, earned income is reduced by the amount of the Keogh contribution. In addition, the individual may contribute to an IRA. This is a phenomenal tax break. Anyone who is qualified should take maximum advantage of a Keogh plan.

There are three approaches to funding such a plan, and the individual must select one of the three. *Fully insured plans* invest in insurance policies, either individual retirement income or annuity policies. They are simple to administer and offer a guaranteed income at a guaranteed rate. A *noninsured* plan is invested by a trustee, usually in mutual funds that have the possibility of equity appreciation. A *split-funded plan* divides the contributions between fixed-income instruments and an equity-building investment fund. Finally, there is the self-directed approach, with the owner of the Keogh deciding how his funds will be invested.

Benefit payout may begin any time between the ages of 59½ and 70½. Premature distributions will lead to income taxation in the year of withdrawal, a 10-percent penalty tax, and disqualification for Keogh participation for five years. The only exception is for disability. Benefits are taxed as ordinary income in the year received, except if a lump-sum distribution is elected, and distributions must begin at age 70½. Distributions to beneficiaries are exempt from federal estate taxes, but will be taxed as ordinary income.

Individual Retirement Accounts

Unless you have been on a desert island or in the Himalayas for the past several years, you are well aware of IRAs. While they had been in existence for some time, it was not until 1981 that eligibility was broadened to include people who were already parties to qualified pension or profit-sharing plans. Since then, they have been widely advertised. The minimum investment in many financial products has been reduced to permit IRA investors to participate. Their popularity is phenomenal, and justifiably so. Let me briefly review their characteristics:

An individual may deposit up to 100 percent of compensation, or $2,000, whichever is less, plus another $250 for a nonworking spouse.

The amount contributed to an IRA is tax-deductible in the year of deposit and accumulates tax-free until withdrawal. This gives the IRA that magic touch of tax-free compounding.

The money may be used to fund an enormous variety of investments. Almost anything goes, except collectibles. And you can split your IRA funds among several accounts for greater diversity and protection.

You may take advantage of tax-free rollovers to transfer your IRA funds between accounts. The rollover provisions also apply to transfers of assets from one qualified plan to another through an IRA account.

IRA assets are exempt from creditors' claims, too. But they can be reached by a spouse in case of divorce.

Let's look at our earlier illustration of tax-free compounding another way. If you save $2,000 per year for the periods listed below, and invest it at 12 percent interest, you will get the following results:

Year	Amount Accumulated
1	$ 2,240
5	14,230
10	39,310
15	83,505
20	161,395
30	540,585
40	1,718,284

Note: Figures based upon $2,000 contributed on January 1 of each year, with annual compounding and an average annual return of 12%. All figures are rounded to the nearest dollar.

These numbers are analogous to what your qualified plan, Keogh, or IRA will earn. The difference between them and what you could otherwise save in a 40-percent tax bracket, for example, is twofold: (1) you could invest only $600 initially for every $1,000 of qualified money *and* (2) you would only receive 60 percent of any interest income—8 percent instead of 12 percent, for example. The combination of the higher base for investment and the higher rate has a tremendous cumulative power.

This cumulative appreciation aspect of these plans argues for making your full maximum legal deposits as early in the calendar year as you can possibly manage, particularly if you have liquid assets in other taxable accounts that could be turned into a tax-free qualified account.

The only drawbacks to an IRA are that you cannot take the money out before age 59½ without penalty, unless you become disabled (it will go to your beneficiary if you die sooner). This may make starting an IRA questionable for very young wage earners with relatively low incomes. If you do make an early withdrawal, try to roll over part of the funds, taking out only what you need. You will pay current income tax and penalties only on the amount you retain.

The second drawback is that you must pay ordinary income tax on the withdrawals whenever you take them. (As with Keoghs, withdrawals must begin no later than age 70½.) But this may be more than offset by the extra interest accrued on your tax-free deposits over the years. Your tax adviser may also have some suggestions for minimizing the tax bite when you begin to withdraw your IRA contributions.

And, of course, there is purchasing-power risk: you can't know how much your savings will buy in the future. But this is true of any long-term investment. On the whole, then, the IRA is aptly called "the workingman's (and working-woman's) tax shelter."

Lump-Sum Distributions

Almost every week, several men and women come to us for help with one of the most important financial decisions of their life—how to take their retirement benefits. Many company pension plans offer two or more alternatives in the manner of payment. The most common are these:

1. A single-life annuity, which provides fixed monthly income for the retiree until his death.
2. A joint-and-survivor annuity, which provides income for the retiree and for his spouse until death if she survives him. Monthly benefits paid under this option are lower than those paid for the retiree alone.
3. A lump-sum payment in lieu of an annuity, determined by a formula based on the actu-arial value of the annuity to which the retiree is entitled.

The choice among these options should be based on careful calculation of the economic results of the choice and the needs and plans of each individual retiree. In most instances, the retirees we see choose the lump-sum option, for a very simple reason. If they take the annuity, nothing remains on the death of the individuals covered under options 1 and 2 above. If they take the lump sum, invest it, and live on the income, the principal will be intact and when they die will benefit their heirs.

If you choose the lump-sum option, you and your tax adviser should examine carefully the tax-deferral and

-avoidance options that are available to you. For tax purposes, the amount you have contributed to the retirement plan is not taxed; the amount contributed to the plan by the company for service prior to 1974 is taxed at the long-term capital-gains rate (current maximum: 20 percent), and the company contribution from 1974 to the date of distribution is taxed at your ordinary income tax rate during the year in which the distribution is made.

However, if you have no immediate need for income, you can roll over part of the lump sum into an IRA or a Keogh plan, if you have one, where it will compound tax-free until you need to begin withdrawing funds. They then will be taxed at your ordinary income tax rate as the funds are withdrawn.

Your second option is to use 10-year forward averaging to reduce the amount of the tax. Essentially, this involves dividing the amount of the lump sum, figuring the tax on the product of this division at the single-taxpayer rate, and then multiplying the amount of tax owed by 10. The amount owed will be substantially less, in most cases, than the amount you would have owed if you simply added the total lump sum to your income for the year.

A number of variables will influence your choice between a rollover or forward averaging. The most signficant are the amount of the rollover and the length of time it can be left in your IRA or Keogh account. If you expect to need income at once, or in the relatively near future, 10-year forward averaging will probably make the most sense. If you do not expect to need income for several years, you may benefit more from the compounding effect of investing the total rollover amount and allowing the interest to compound tax-deferred. In any case, the choice is not one you can make without seeking the help of a competent tax adviser to run the numbers on the alternatives and compare the results.

If a lump-sum distribution is made to the beneficiary of a deceased employee, the estate must choose between an exclusion of the lump sum for federal estate tax purposes or 10-year averaging for income tax purposes. One or the other must be waived. Every case is different, so you must get competent assistance.

If you fail to handle retirement correctly, you can lose a lot of money and be very sorry. This can happen even to ostensibly sophisticated people, like the $110,000-a-year executive we helped recently. He faced involuntary retirement at age fifty-eight. His company extended his health insurance coverage for five years and told him how much monthly income he would receive, but neglected to mention that he was also entitled to a lump-sum distribution. The amount was $127,000.

Until we explained this to him, he had no idea he was being cheated. Only when he understood the situation and its consequences could he go back to his employer and demand what he had every right to. The point of the story is that you must be aware of what is rightfully yours, and for complicated matters like pension benefits your best course of action may be to seek competent, seasoned outside professional counsel.

CHAPTER 15

ESTATE PLANNING

In one sense, this is the culmination of all your planning and investment efforts. In another sense, it is an ongoing task, the ramifications of which should be part of every financial decision you make throughout life. Its primary goal is congruent with that of all financial planning: to ensure your own security and that of those you care most about. But in estate planning, the added goal is to provide for the financial security of others even after your death. It is a solemn responsibility, and a complex one, which will be with you for a lifetime if you give it the attention it deserves. Your aim should be to bring together on your behalf a team of seasoned professionals whose judgment you trust, and to become knowledgeable yourself.

As always, you must know your own objectives and you must take action. Your objectives may include choosing executors and trustees, planning how to distribute your property (both during your lifetime and after your death), providing sufficient financial support for your dependents, assuring adequate liquidity to meet estate obligations, planning the disposal of closely held business interests, and reducing death expenses to a minimum. Taking action includes determining the current size of your estate, what taxes would be due, and whether some could be avoided. And then it means writing a will, buying enough life insurance, and setting up trusts if appropriate.

Insurance and Liquidity

Especially if you are relatively young and have dependents, make certain that you are adequately insured. Insurance gives your family an "instant estate" to rely on in the event of your death. Generally speaking, the death benefits from insurance pass outside the estate and are also not subject to income tax.

Insurance is equally important for a whole or part owner of a closely held business, as will be discussed later in the chapter.

A crucial function of insurance in estate planning is the liquidity it provides. If most of your assets are in nonliquid forms, such as a house with a mortgage or a small business, insurance could make the difference between a comfortable amount of money to pay taxes, administration expenses, and other adjustment costs—and a forced sale of assets to meet those death expenses.

You Need a Will

I'm not given to making absolute statements, but in this case I shall. You *must* have a will. If you are married, do not assume that if you die, your wife or husband will get everything. The unfortunate fact is that under the laws of intestacy in many states, your spouse may be entitled to only one-third of your estate, or to an equal share with each of your children. Even worse (and not unimaginable for a younger couple), you and your spouse may die in a common disaster.

In either case, your estate would have to be administered by the courts. This includes the appointment of a guardian, who may or may not be the surviving parent, for your minor children. A court-appointed guardian must be paid a fee, and there will be other costs that will reduce the value of your estate.

Similarly if you are single. Perhaps you help support elderly parents or a disabled relative, while your equally comfortable siblings shirk this responsibility. Would you want them to share your estate with your needy parent or other relative? A will could set up a trust, administered by a corporate trustee or an individual of your choice, for such a person's care. You may have minor children from a previous marriage, or by adoption, who need the entire proceeds of your estate—not just the portion that doesn't go to your wealthy brother and your spendthrift niece. Or you have an extremely close friend or roommate, or a charity in which you are active that means a great deal to you. They will receive nothing unless you provide for it before your death.

The point is that while state laws and court administration are generally as fair as can reasonably be expected, they were nevertheless designed to deal with *all* intestate successions, *not* with the specifics of your situation. The brutal fact is that *you cannot afford to be without a will.*

As we proceed with the discussion in this chapter, I will point out some elements that your will should govern, and some it may not. In outline, a will should include at least the following information:

Date will executed; *Prepared by* whom

Specific bequests: personal property, money bequests, charitable bequests, business interests, residence and real estate

Distribution of the remainder: outright or in trust, provisions and distributions, and to whom— spouse, children, others (including contingent beneficiaries)

Fiduciaries: executor, successor executors, trustees and
   successors, guardians, and successor guardians of
   minor children or incompetents

Choosing Your Fiduciaries

In some ways, this is as important a task as completing
the will itself. The people you choose to execute your wishes
as expressed in the will must be utterly trustworthy, reliable, and savvy. As fiduciaries, they must have no other
agenda than serving the best interests of your heirs. Indeed,
they are legally bound to do so.

If they are what they should be, you can give them broad
discretion to select options or alter the specifics of your bequests: to change investments, dispose of business interests,
retain or dispose of real estate or other property, and borrow or lend money. This flexibility will enable them to deal
with changing circumstances you cannot foresee, and still
meet your overriding long-term goals.

Some of these individuals may be the same ones who
help you fashion your estate plan and carry it out: your
attorney, accountant, insurance agent, banker or trust officer, broker, or other financial advisers. Others may not.
Whomever you choose, they must be people in whom you
have total confidence and trust.

As a minimum, you will need an *executor,* who is responsible for carrying out the provisions of your will, and one
or more *trustees* to administer any trusts you may set up
either during your life or upon your death (see section on
trusts). The executor's duties include assembling your property; managing, safekeeping, and insuring it during the settlement period; paying expenses and taxes; and distributing
the net proceeds to your heirs. For these tasks and their
advice to your heirs, the executor is entitled to reasonable
compensation—although a family member or friend may

waive it. In the case of a bank, the commission would be a sliding percentage scale, based on the gross estate value, with a minimum of several thousand dollars a year.

If you have minor children, you must also have a *guardian* of their person and a guardian of their property (not necessarily the same person or institution).

You may choose either individual or corporate fiduciaries, such as a bank trust department, for most of the roles (guardians of the person of a minor child is an obvious exception; this must be an individual who loves the child). For some purposes, the continuity and professional management available from a corporate fiduciary will more than offset the fees charged. Finally (at least for individuals), always name *contingent fiduciaries,* as you would contingent beneficiaries, to guard against the death, disability, or refusal to serve of your initial selections.

What Is Your Estate?

The short answer is "that depends." Your *probate estate* is the property that is disposed of by will, whether you own it outright, in common with others, or in the form of life insurance payable to your estate. This property may be attached by creditors or contested by unhappy heirs apparent, and will have administration costs and settlement delays. But these drawbacks must be weighed against the disadvantages of giving up ownership and control of your property before you die.

Your *gross estate* is defined by tax law and used as the starting point for calculations of estate tax owed. It includes:

1. probate estate property,
2. half the value of property owned jointly with a spouse and all the value of property owned

jointly with another party (unless that person can show an independent contribution to the purchase of the property),

3. any life insurance (i.e., the cash value of the insurance itself, not the death benefit) owned on one's own life.

Gross estate may also include certain gifts made "in contemplation of death" within the last three years of life, especially of life insurance, and property over which you have powers of appointment or in which you retain partial interests or rights.

Deductions and credits against the gross estate (discussed in detail below) yield the adjusted gross estate, to which other deductions apply, leading to the *taxable estate*.

The *distributable estate* is what is left after federal estate taxes, state death taxes (if any), payment of current debts, and funeral and administration expenses.

Tax Planning for Your Estate

Estate erosion is what taxes and other costs can do to reduce the size of the distributable estate. If you think of estate planning as the *conservation* of what you have accumulated and its transfer to your beneficiaries, then your objective is to maximize your distributable estate. This section is a very brief and necessarily incomplete overview of tax considerations that will help you avoid unnecessary tax erosion. One of its omissions is its failure to cover state death and inheritance taxes. Most states have one or the other. Some have both. They are all different. So you must seek the guidance of knowledgeable tax advisers in your geographic area to handle this aspect of your tax planning.

That said, let us deal with federal taxes. These were changed radically in the 1981 Tax Act. If you have a will which predates that act, it is imperative that you have it updated.

Unified Gift and Estate Tax

Many people are unaware of the fact that there are gift taxes. There are, and they may be important. Under current law, you may give gifts of valuable property to any individual, of up to $10,000 per year. If you are married, your combined gift to any individual may be up to $20,000. This may sound like a great deal and seem unlikely to be exceeded. Let's say, for example, that you own a successful small business and want to transfer it during your lifetime to your children. Then these numbers suddenly seem smaller.

As of 1986, the unified estate and gift tax credit is $155,000, meaning up to $500,000 of your estate plus taxable gifts is tax-free. For 1987 and subsequent years, the credit rises to $192,800, for a tax-free base of $600,000. Above that amount, gifts above the annual exclusion plus the taxable estate are subject to the unified gift and estate tax, a single progressive-rate schedule ranging from 37 to 50 percent.

What this all boils down to is that if you have made no gifts in excess of the $10,000-per-person annual exclusion, you can leave a net estate of up to $600,000 free of the federal estate tax.

Unlimited Marital Deduction

This is another new wrinkle since 1981. If you are married, you may leave your entire estate—or whatever portion—to your surviving spouse, and pay *no* federal estate tax. You may also give gifts of any amount to your spouse during your lifetime without paying gift tax.

This may sound wonderful, but there is a catch. Unless

your estate is small and your wife or husband has no other property, the surviving spouse's estate (which will not have the advantage of the marital deduction unless the survivor remarries) may get clobbered with taxes upon his or her death.

This is a problem primarily for estates in the $600,000–$1.2-million range. Below that range, there should be no federal tax due. Above it, there will almost always be some tax on the second estate, although many devices may be used to minimize the bite. The danger for people with estates in the middle range is that they will "overqualify" the estate of the first spouse in terms of the marital deduction, leaving too much to shelter in the estate of the second.

We know that estates up to $600,000 are not subject to estate tax anyway. Given that fact, the wisest course may be to remove property totaling approximately that amount from the estate, perhaps by placing it in a so-called non-marital trust (which is set up to be ineligible for the deduction), and to claim the marital deduction for the remainder. This minimizes the size of the second spouse's taxable estate. Another alternative is to leave the remainder in trust for the survivor (see the trust section, p. 187) with a life income, so that it does not pass through his or her estate.

Generation-skipping Transfers

People who are fortunate enough to have substantial estates may find themselves in the awkward, though enviable, position of having their most obvious potential heirs too affluent to be benefited by outright bequests of property. It is common in this case to put some property in trust with a life interest for the well-off spouse or adult child, the property itself passing to another after the beneficiary's death. This has the effect of "skipping" estates, so the property passes to a less-wealthy individual.

Since the 1976 Tax Act there has been a tax on such generation-skipping transfers. The tax operates by treating the principal of the trust as taxable to the estate of the intervening beneficiary (called the "deemed transferor") on his or her death. There is one important exclusion: it applies to grandchildren. Generation-skipping transfers that are vested to them are taxable only to the extent that they exceed $250,000 for each deemed transferor or intervening beneficiary.

For example, if you have two daughters, each of whom has children of her own, you could pass through a total of $500,000 to your grandchildren without estate tax. The maximum amount that could go to each grandchild would depend on how many children each daughter has. If one daughter has one child and the other has three, the single child could get up to $250,000 and the threesome would have to split that amount. (Of course, nothing requires you to give the maximum amount.) If each daughter has two children, each grandchild could get up to $125,000 tax-free.

The "Preview"

Situations like this point up the need for careful tax planning to help you make the appropriate decisions. Unless this is handled correctly, you could end up paying too much tax. What is needed is a review or trial run of your estate plan and tax options to see what will work best. That means making an inventory of your assets, estimating how they would be taxed if you took no further action, and seeing what additional tax-saving steps you can take if you are dissatisfied with the initial results.

You should also consider what property passes inside your will and what property outside it, to be sure your master plan is comprehensive and that your will produces the intended results. Even if you design an estate plan in which none of your property passes through your will, you must still have the document to deal with residual property not otherwise mentioned, and to provide for alternate distributions or contingent beneficiaries if needed. Finally, if you are married, go through the exercise of assuming a reversal in the anticipated order of deaths to see if both wills would still produce the results you want.

Of course, all this is a lot of work. But it is what planning is all about: doing the spadework necessary to avoid unforeseen and unpleasant consequences—like overpaying your estate taxes.

If you and your estate-planning team do this step well, and follow up by implementing any needed changes, you may find that you have a distributable estate, much of which is free from taxation. Here are some examples of nontaxable property: your spouse's half of jointly owned property, pension benefits payable to an outside beneficiary (not your estate), insurance on your life owned by someone else, and a living trust to remove property from estate taxes.

About Trusts

These useful estate-planning vehicles have already been mentioned. Let's look at them more closely and see what they're about.

A trust is a fiduciary arrangement you can set up as the grantor or creator, whereby you give a trustee legal title to property you place in the trust. The trustee is required to manage the property for the benefit of a third party, the person who holds the equitable title to the property or trust beneficiary. The creator or settlor is empowered to set all conditions of the trust: its duration, what the beneficiaries must do to receive it, if anything, its alternate disposition if conditions are not met, and what discretion the trustee may use.

For example, suppose you place an income-yielding piece of real estate in trust with the local bank's trust department, making the income payable to your married daughter for her life and naming her three children to receive the property jointly upon her death. Your daughter is called the life tenant and her interest a life estate. Your grandchildren, who receive nothing until their mother's death, are called "remaindermen" and their interest a remainder interest.

The creator may name him- or herself trustee, but runs the risk of adverse tax consequence. As with executors, individual or corporate trustees may be chosen. Carefully consider the merits of professional management, technical expertise, continuity, independence, and lack of bias that professional trustees offer in exchange for their fees. Professional trustees usually charge annual fees based on the value of the trust corpus (principal) or its income, plus a commission on principal distributions.

Trusts are tremendously flexible instruments that can serve any number of estate-planning objectives. They have many forms, the most important of which for our purposes are *inter vivos,* or living trusts, and *testamentary trusts* created by a will.

Living Trusts

The trust described in the example above is an inter vivos trust that goes into effect during your lifetime. Living trusts are of two major types: irrevocable and revocable. *Irrevocable trusts* cannot be terminated, and they offer tax advantages. You will not have to pay any income tax on the trust's income if it meets certain conditions: you cannot receive any of the income, and it cannot be accumulated to benefit you or your spouse, to buy insurance on either of your lives, or to discharge any of your legal obligations (including the obligation to support a minor child). Furthermore, if you transfer assets to an irrevocable trust with no strings attached, it is considered a completed gift and removed from your taxable estate.

Of course, you must relinquish all ownership powers in the property that forms the trust corpus, a matter for serious thought. On the other hand, this loss of use may be balanced by a potential extension of control. In the example discussed above, for instance, you would control the disposition of your property throughout your daughter's lifetime and beyond (presumably beyond your own as well).

Revocable trusts do not have the same constraints; nor do they have the same tax benefits. They simply enable the creator to turn the management of his or her assets over to the trustee. This may be advantageous, for example, to the entrepreneurial owner of a small business who is contemplating retirement. By naming herself as beneficiary, she can continue to receive income from the business, while the trustee is responsible for locating successor management and operating the business.

An important group of living trusts are *insurance trusts*, in which at least part of the trust corpus consists of life insurance. An *unfunded* trust has insurance policies alone, or is named as beneficiary of life insurance policies payable at death. A *funded* insurance trust also contains other assets, the income from which is used to pay the insurance premiums. Since the trust is a separate tax entity with a lower tax bracket than its creator, the net income will be higher and can purchase more coverage. Irrevocable insurance trusts also avoid estate taxes because the insurance cash value is considered as a gift at the time it is assigned. Premium payments are also considered gifts.

More frequently, insurance trusts are revocable. This gives

greater flexibility and assures the grantor that his objectives will be carried out at his death. This use of a revocable insurance trust may be particularly important in instances where insurance proceeds will constitute a large proportion of the individual's estate but he or she feels an outright lump-sum payment might be poorly managed.

Either type of insurance trust has advantages over payment of the proceeds directly to the estate: the proceeds are not subject to creditors, they are often exempt from state taxes, they are not part of the probate estate so administrative costs are avoided, and they are immediately liquid. Leaving the proceeds in trust, as you might do in the case where the beneficiaries are minor children, also permits greater flexibility and control than using the settlement options offered by the insurance company. On the other hand, the insurance companies would argue that they charge no direct fees, that settlement options guarantee both principal and income, and that annuity options are available only from them. The decision is yours.

The Short-term or Clifford Trust

This is a device for high-bracket taxpayers. It involves diverting income from some of one's property to others who are in lower tax brackets. An irrevocable trust lasting at least ten years before it reverts to the creator is not taxed on his income tax return during that time. If the income is paid to the beneficiary, it is taxed to the beneficiary; if allowed to accumulate, it is taxed to the trust. The transfer of the ten-year interest in the property is a gift, subject to gift tax if its value is above the annual $10,000 exclusion. To get the benefits of a Clifford trust, the grantor must give up the rights of enjoyment of the property for the duration, and cannot use its income to support anyone the law requires him to support anyway—a spouse or a minor child.

One way to use this kind of trust is to provide for the

support of an indigent parent. A 50-percent income-tax payer needs to earn twice the amount he or she wishes to contribute to a parent's support. By creating a trust for the parent's benefit and placing property in it which will yield the appropriate amount, the income will be taxed at the parent's lower marginal rate. The trust can also be made to run for the parent's lifetime, continuing the support if the grantor were to die first or if the parent lives more than another ten years. At the end, the trust corpus reverts to the grantor or the grantor's estate.

Testamentary Trusts

These are trusts created by your will. They have the same variety of forms as inter vivos trusts. Used in conjunction with a power of appointment, a testamentary trust permits the trustee the flexibility to manage unforeseen situations appropriately. Property can also be added to a previously created living trust upon your death (as in the case of an unfunded insurance trust, above), a process known as "pouring over." The use of trusts rather than outright bequests is a matter of discretion that depends totally on your personal objectives and circumstances. Certainly they are useful for minor beneficiaries or incompetents, for keeping certain assets whole, and in any situation where professional management is needed. A few examples are listed below.

The qualified terminable interest property, or Q-TIP, trust applies to property that passes to a surviving spouse in trust, with the trust income payable irrevocably to him or her for life. After the survivor's death, the property passes to the person designated in the decedent's will. A Q-TIP trust can serve as the marital portion in an estate that is divided between marital and nonmarital trusts to avoid overqualifying an estate for the marital deduction.

Sprinkling trusts are another special device which can use the flexibility of the trust instrument to meet unforeseeable needs or to reduce overall family taxes. The will permits the trustee to "sprinkle" or "spray" the trust's income among a group of beneficiaries at his discretion. (This device can also be used with living trusts.)

Charitable Gifts or Bequests

As you develop your estate plan, don't overlook the benefits that may be obtained from charitable giving. Helping those less fortunate is always a source of personal satisfaction, and may yield significant tax advantages, as well. Your gifts may be in the form of donations made from current income directly to qualified nonprofit organizations whose goals appeal to you. Also worth investigating is the creation of a trust for charitable purposes, or the possibility of making a charitable bequest. Since any form of philanthropy is tax-benefited, choose the timing that serves your estate-planning needs best: do you need a way to save estate taxes or income taxes?

One caveat: be sure the organization you intend to shower with your largesse is qualified to receive tax-deductible contributions. Not all nonprofit organizations are. Ask to see a copy of their 501(c)(3) designation from the IRS if you have any doubts.

You can benefit a charity through a trust in any of a number of ways. For example, the *charitable income trust* funnels the income from the trust to the charity, while the property or corpus remains yours or your beneficiary's. You can use a short-term trust for this purpose very effectively. Another type is the *charitable remainder trust*. This is almost the converse of the income trust: you give the property to the charity in trust but retain the right to a lifetime income from the corpus for yourself or your beneficiary. Upon your death, the charity disposes of the property as it wishes; it will not pass through your estate. You can also establish an *insurance trust* to benefit a charity while maximizing your tax deductions.

You may also want to consider establishing a private charitable foundation of your own, either upon your death or during your lifetime. This can be particularly effective if a closely held business is a major asset. By reorganizing the capital structure of the firm and placing part of it in a foundation, it may be possible to reduce estate taxes and improve liquidity. This is quite complicated, however, and has many tax ramifications best explored by experts.

Disposition of Closely Held Business Interest

For many people, an operating business is not only their life's work, but also their major asset. Those people have another set of reasons for careful planning, for insurance, and for a will: to preserve the business or its value for their heirs. If the business is a partnership or a small corporation, the loss of one of the partners may have severe adverse effects on it, either as a going concern or as a prospect for acquisition. Your responsibility to your partner or partners, as well as to your family, is to minimize this adversity through preparation.

If you have a close corporation, you and fellow stockholders should hold insurance on one another's lives, in conjunction with a buy-sell agreement. Such an agreement sets forth an asking price for the business in advance and gives its principals first rights to buy out one another's interests at that price. In the event that one of the partners dies, the others have both the right (provided by the buy-sell agreement) and the liquidity (provided by the insurance policy) to buy out his share. In the absence of such an agreement, your family could find itself uncomfortably in business with your colleagues, or the latter could be forced to liquidate the business as trustees for your heirs. Neither outcome is desirable.

If you are a sole proprietor, you must provide for the disposition of your business by living transfer or by will. Look realistically at your business: could it continue to prosper without you? If not, your family's security may be at risk when you die.

You must consider the possibility of a sale, perhaps to your key personnel on an installment basis, commencing during your lifetime. If you are lucky, you have family members who could be groomed to succeed you and are interested in the business. Inform them of your goals, begin immediately to prepare them for management responsibilities, and perhaps begin to transfer ownership through gifts. In either case, this method has the advantage of removing the business from your taxable estate, but the drawback of subjecting you to capital-gains taxes. Perhaps a larger company would be interested in acquiring your business through an exchange of stock, which avoids immediate capital gains. Or there may be interest in a sale tied to a management or consulting contract for your services.

In a family business where not all family members participate actively, you must find a way to treat both groups fairly. One possibility is to divide the income among all family members through issuing preferred stock, but keep the equity and management control in the hands of the active participant(s), who would hold the common stock. Other such solutions can be found to meet your own situation. What you wish to avoid at all costs is a forced liquidation of the business after your death to meet the demands of creditors, pay taxes, and handle administration expenses. This can be done with "key executive" insurance or a sinking fund. If the value of the business exceeds 35 percent of the adjusted gross estate, the company can do a "section 303" stock redemption to pay death expenses, including estate taxes; or it may use the installment method and take up to fifteen years to pay its share of estate taxes. (Other conditions apply; consult your tax adviser.)

Valuation of your business for tax purposes can be a tricky proposition. The IRS considers a number of factors; you might be well-advised to familiarize yourself with them. Also consider getting a professional appraisal. A preexisting part-nership or stockholders' agreement, buy-sell agreement, or option to purchase at a particular price will determine the value for estate-tax purposes.

CHAPTER 16

CONCLUSION: PUTTING IT ALL TOGETHER

While the specifics of the preceding pages may be complicated, the main message of this book is simple: Stop drifting and dreaming! Find out where you are and know where you want to go. Take control of your money so you can have what you want in your life. We have seen how, through planning and prudent action, even the most expensive goals can be met.

As you plan your investment program, start by paying yourself first. Remember that everything you do with your money is an investment, and that the quality of investment is as important as the rate of return. I have stressed the virtues of consistency and patience in choosing your investments and in carrying out your plans. I have consistently urged you to seek advisers of excellence and integrity, establish ongoing relationships with them, and learn from their expertise.

I have also covered a wide variety of investment possibilities and pointed out winners that can work for you whether your aim is capital appreciation, current income, or tax shelter. This review has pointed out that some types of investments are losers pure and simple, whereas other can be winners if they are used correctly. For example:

Savings accounts and bank CDs are generally losers or

noninvestment investments, although you must keep at least three months of income in highly liquid form to guard against emergencies.

Mutual funds are losers if they are poorly managed, fail to meet your investment criteria, or (for money-market funds) if interest rates are low, *but* if they have good track records, and your timing is right, they can be the ideal vehicle for investing in foreign stocks, government securities, or gold.

Common stocks are generally too volatile to guarantee preservation of capital, *unless* you guard against a precipitous drop in price with a stop-loss order or a put hedge.

Most coupon bonds are losers because of interest rate, liquidity, and inflation risks, *but* taxable zero-coupon bonds can be winners if used in custodial accounts or qualified pension plans.

Whatever your personal investment objectives, you want to maximize your total return consistent with your tolerance for risk. Seek value for your money and management quality. Evaluate the tradeoffs among investment alternatives and learn to recognize the right investments for you. When you make a mistake, acknowledge it quickly and cut your losses short. But let your profits ride. A balanced portfolio of safe, low-risk, winning investments is the best way to meet a variety of investment objectives.

When security is paramount and accumulated wealth is low, manage risks with insurance. Later, as you prepare for retirement, know your entitlements, but also use tax-benefited low-risk vehicles like IRAs, conservative limited partnerships, and deferred annuities. Such investments, which you undertake independently, can guarantee you a comfortable retirement on your own. Learn to use trusts and other devices effectively to conserve and transfer your estate intact, thus ensuring the continued financial well-being of those you love after your death.

This brief summary of key points should remind you once again of the importance of planning and taking action to meet your goals. So don't stop when you reach the end of this page. Use this book as your guide, analyze your objectives, and start putting your financial plan into effect NOW. If you are confused about any of the concepts I have presented, don't hesitate to ask for help. Call me collect at (312) 435-4882, and I'll try to answer your questions.

If you're serious about your money, and willing to work at managing it, you *can* become rich without risk!

GLOSSARY

Every technical field has a language of its own, which is not always comprehensible to nonprofessional audiences. To the extent possible, I have tried to avoid financial gobbledygook in this book, but some use of technical terms was unavoidable, and there are others not used that you may encounter as you pursue your financial plan. This glossary is included as a quick reference for readers who seek a more precise definition of some of the terms.

ACCRUED INTEREST   Interest accrued on a bond since the last payment was made. The buyer of the bond pays the market price plus accrued interest. Exceptions include bonds that are in default and income bonds. (*See* Flat; Income Bond)

AMORTIZATION   Accounting for expenses or charges as applicable rather than as paid. Includes such practices as depreciation, depletion, write-off of intangibles, prepaid expenses, and deferred charges. In the case of the Dow Jones Industrial Average, the prices of the thirty stocks are totaled and then divided by a divisor intended to compensate for past stock splits and stock dividends and changes from time to time. As a result, point changes in the average have only the vaguest relationship to dollar

199

price changes in stocks included in the average. Currently, the divisor is 1,598, so that a one-point change in the industrial average is actually the equivalent of 5.3 cents. (*See* NYSE Common; Point; Split)

AVERAGING   (*See* Dollar Cost Averaging)

BALANCE SHEET   A condensed financial statement showing the nature and amount of a company's assets, liabilities, and capital on a given date. In dollar amounts the balance sheet shows what the company owns, what it owes, and the ownership interest in the company of its stockholders. (*See* Earnings Report)

BASIS BOOK   A book of mathematical tables used to convert yield percentages to equivalent dollar prices.

BASIS PRICE   The price expressed in yield or net return on the investment.

BEAR   Someone who believes the market will decline. (*See* Bull)

BEAR MARKET   A declining market. (*See* Bull Market)

BEARER BOND   A bond that does not have the owner's name registered on the books of the issuing company and that is payable to the holder. (*See* Coupon Bond; Registered Bond)

BID AND ASKED   Often referred to as a quotation or quote. The bid is the highest price anyone has declared he wants to pay for a security at a given time, and the asked is the lowest price anyone will take at the same time. (*See* Quotation)

BIG BOARD   A popular term for the New York Stock Exchange.

BLOCK   A large holding or transaction of stock, popularly considered to be 10,000 shares or more.

BLUE CHIP   A company known nationally for the quality and wide acceptance of its products or services, and for its ability to make money and pay dividends.

BLUE SKY LAWS   A popular name of laws various states have enacted to protect the public against securities frauds. The term is believed to have originated when a judge ruled a particular stock has about the same value as a patch of blue sky.

BOARD ROOM   A room for registered representatives and customers in a broker's office where opening, high, low, and last prices of leading stocks used to be posted on a board throughout the market day. Today such price displays are normally electronically controlled, although most board rooms have replaced the board with the ticker and/or individual quotation machines.

BOND   Basically an IOU or promissory note of a corporation, usually issued in multiples of $1,000 or $5,000, although $100 and $500 denominations are not unknown. A bond is evidence of a debt on which the issuing company usually promises to pay the bondholders a specified amount of interest for a specified length of time and to repay the loan on the expiration date. In every case a bond represents debt—its holder is a creditor of the corporation and not a part owner, as is the shareholder. In most cases, bonds are secured by a mortgage.

(*See* Collateral Trust Bond; Convertible; Debenture; General Mortgage Bond; Income Bond)

BOOK   A notebook the specialist in a stock uses to keep a record of the buy-and-sell orders at specified prices, in sequence of receipt, that are left with him by other brokers. (*See* Specialist)

BOOK VALUE   An accounting term. Book value of a stock is determined from a company's records by adding all assets (generally excluding such intangibles as goodwill), then deducting all debts and other liabilities, plus the liquidation price of any preferred issues. The sum arrived at is divided by the number of common shares outstanding and the result is book value per common share. Book value of the assets of a company or a security may have little or no significant relationship to market value.

BROKER   An agent who handles the public's orders to buy and sell securities, commodities, or other property. For this service a commission is charged. (*See* Commission Broker; Dealer)

BROKERS' LOANS   Money borrowed by brokers from banks for a variety of uses. It may be used by specialists and odd-lot dealers to help finance inventories of stock they deal in; by brokerage firms to finance the underwriting of new issues of corporate and municipal securities; to help finance a firm's own investments; and to help finance the purchase of securities for customers who prefer to use the broker's credit when they buy securities. (*See* Margin)

BULL   One who believes the market will rise. (*See* Bear)

BULL MARKET   An advancing market. (*See* Bear Market)

CALL   (*See* Option)

CALLABLE   A bond issue, all or part of which may be redeemed by the issuing corporation under definite conditions before maturity. The term also applies to preferred
shares redeemable by the issuing corporation.

CAPITAL GAIN OR CAPITAL LOSS   Profit or loss from the sale
of a capital asset. A capital gain, under current federal
income tax laws, may be either short-term (12 months
or less) or long-term (more than 12 months). A short-
term capital gain is taxed at the reporting individual's
full income tax rate. A long-term capital gain is subject
to a lower tax. The capital-gains provisions of the tax
law are complicated. You should consult your tax adviser for specific information.

CAPITAL STOCK   All shares representing ownership of a
business, including preferred and common stock. (*See*
Common Stock; Preferred Stock)

CAPITALIZATION   Total amount of the various securities issued by a corporation. Capitalization may include bonds,
debentures, preferred and common stock, and surplus.
Bonds and debentures are usually carried on the books
of the issuing company in terms of their par or face value.
Preferred and common shares may be carried in terms of
par or stated value. Stated value may be an arbitrary figure decided upon by the directors or may represent the
amount received by the company from the sale of the
securities at the time of issuance. (*See* Par)

CASH FLOW   Reported net income of a corporation plus amounts charged off for depreciation, depletion, amortization, and extraordinary charges to reserves, which are bookkeeping deductions and not paid out in actual dollars and cents. (*See* Amortization; Depletion; Depreciation)

CASH SALE   A transaction on the floor of the Stock Exchange calling for delivery of the securities the same day. In "regular-way" trades, the seller is to deliver on the fifth business day.

CERTIFICATE   The actual piece of paper that is evidence of ownership of stock in a corporation. Watermarked paper is finely engraved with delicate etchings to discourage forgery. Loss of a certificate may at the least cause a great deal of inconvenience and, at the worst, financial loss.

COLLATERAL   Securities or other property pledged by a borrower to secure repayment of a loan.

COLLATERAL TRUST BOND   A bond secured by collateral deposited with a trustee. The collateral is often the stocks or bonds of companies controlled by the issuing company, but may be other securities.

COMMISSION   The broker's basic fee for purchasing or selling securities or property as an agent. The New York Stock Exchange fixes minimum commission rates for orders to purchase or sell NYSE listed stocks when the money involved is more than $2,000 and does not exceed $300,000. Commissions are established independently by each firm for orders up to $2,000 and portions of orders over $300,000.

COMMISSION BROKER   An agent who executes the public's orders for the purchase or sale of securities or commodities.

COMMON STOCK   Securities representing an ownership interest in a corporation. If the company has also issued preferred stock, both common and preferred have ownership rights. The preferred normally is limited to a fixed dividend, but has prior claim on dividends and, in the event of liquidation, assets. Claims of both common and preferred stockholders are junior to claims of bondholders or other creditors of the company. Common stockholders assume the greater risk, but generally exercise the greater control and may gain the greater reward in the form of dividends and capital appreciation. The terms *common stock* and *capital stock* are often used interchangeably when the company has no preferred stock.

CONGLOMERATE   A corporation that has diversified its operations, usually by acquiring enterprises in widely varied industries.

CONSOLIDATED BALANCE SHEET   A balance sheet showing the financial condition of a corporation and its subsidiaries. (*See* Balance Sheet)

CONVERTIBLE   A bond, debenture, or preferred share that may be exchanged by the owner for common stock or another security, usually of the same company, in accordance with the terms of the issue.

CORRESPONDENT   A securities firm, bank, or other financial organization that regularly performs services for another in a place or market to which the other does not have direct access. Securities firms may have correspondents in foreign countries or on exchanges of which they are not members. Correspondents are frequently linked by private wires. Member organizations of the NYSE with offices in New York City may also act as correspondents for out-of-town member organizations which do not maintain New York City offices.

COUPON BOND   Bond with interest coupons attached. The coupons are clipped as they come due and are presented by the holder for payment of interest. (*See* Bearer Bond; Registered Bond)

COVERAGE   A term usually connected with revenue bonds. It is a ratio of net revenues pledged to principal and interest payments to debt-service requirements. It is one of the factors used in evaluating the quality of an issue.

COVERING   Buying a security previously sold short. (*See* Short Sale; Short Covering)

CUMULATIVE PREFERRED   A stock having a provision that if one or more dividends are omitted, the omitted dividends must be paid on the company's common stock.

CUMULATIVE VOTING   A method of voting for corporate directors enabling the shareholder to multiply the number of his shares by the number of directorships being voted on and cast the total for one director or a selected group of directors. A ten-share holder normally casts ten votes for each of, say, twelve nominees to the board of directors. He thus has 120 votes. Under the cumulative voting principals he may do that or he may cast 120 (10 × 12) votes for only one nominee, sixty for two, forty for three, or any other distribution he chooses. Cumulative voting is required under the corporate laws of some states, and is permitted in most others.

CURB EXCHANGE   Former name of the American Stock Exchange, second largest exchange in the country. The term comes from the market's origin on a street in downtown New York.

CURRENT ASSETS   Those assets of a company reasonably expected to be realized in cash, or sold, or consumed during the normal operating cycle of the business. These include cash, U.S. Government bonds, receivables and money due usually within one year, and inventories.

CURRENT LIABILITIES   Money owed and payable by a company, usually within one year.

CUSTOMERS' MAN   (*See* Registered Representative)

DAY ORDER   An order to buy or sell which, if not executed, expires at the end of the trading day on which it was entered.

DEALER   An individual or firm in the securities business acting as a principal rather than as an agent. Typically, a dealer buys for his own account and sells to a customer from his own inventory. The dealer's profit or loss is the difference between the price he pays and the price he receives for the same security. The dealer's confirmation must disclose to his customer that he has acted as principal. The same individual or firm may function, at different times, either as broker or dealer.

DEBENTURE   A promissory note backed by the general credit of a company and usually not secured by a mortgage or lien on any specific property.

DEBIT BALANCE   Portion of purchase price of stock, bonds, or commodities covered by credit extended by a broker to margin customers.

DEBIT LIMIT   The statutory or constituted maximum debt that a municipality can legally incur.

DEBT SERVICE   Required payments for interest on and retirement of principal amount of a debt.

DEFAULT   Failure to pay principal or interest promptly when due or failure to meet indenture provisions.

DENOMINATION   The face amount or par value of a security that the issuer promises to pay on the maturity date. Most municipal bonds are issued with a minimum denomination of $5,000, although a few older issues are available in $1,000 denominations.

DEPLETION   Natural resources, such as metals, oil and gas, and timber, which conceivably can be reduced to zero over the years, present a special problem in capital management. Depletion in an accounting practice consists of charges against earnings based upon the amount of the asset taken out of the total reserves in the period for which accounting is made. A bookkeeping entry, it does not represent any cash outlay, nor are any funds earmarked for the purpose.

DEPOSITORY TRUST COMPANY (DTC)   A central securities-certificate depository through which members effect security deliveries between each other via computerized bookkeeping entries, thereby reducing the physical movement of stock certificates.

DEPRECIATION   Normally, charges against earnings to write off the cost, less salvage value, of an asset over its estimated useful life. It is a bookkeeping entry and does not represent any cash outlay, and no funds are earmarked for the purpose.

DIRECTOR   Person elected by shareholders to establish company policies. The directors appoint the president, vice presidents, and all other operating officers. Directors decide, among other matters, if and when dividends shall be paid. (*See* Management; Proxy)

DISCOUNT   The amount by which a preferred stock or bond may sell below its par value. Also used as a verb to mean "takes into account" as the price of the stock has discounted the expected dividend cut. (*See* Premium)

DISCRETIONARY ACCOUNT   An account in which the customer gives the broker or someone else discretion, which may be complete or within specific limits, as to the purchase and sale of securities or commodities, including selection, timing, amount, and price to be paid or received.

DIVERSIFICATION   Spreading investments among different companies in different fields. Another type of diversification is also offered by the securities of many individual companies because of the wide range of their activities.

DIVIDEND   The payment designated by the Board of Directors to be distributed pro rata among the shares outstanding. On preferred shares, it is generally a fixed amount. On common shares, the dividend varies with the fortunes of the company and the amount of cash on hand, and may be omitted if business is poor or the directors determine to withhold earnings to invest in plant and equipment. Sometimes a company will pay a dividend out of past earnings even if it is not currently operating at a profit.

DOLLAR BOND   A bond that is quoted and traded in dollars rather than yield.

DOLLAR COST AVERAGING   A system of buying securities at regular intervals with a fixed-dollar amount. Under this system the investor buys by the dollars' worth rather than by the number of shares. If each investment is of the same number of dollars, payments buy more when the price is low and fewer when it rises. Thus, temporary downswings in price benefit the investor if he continues periodic purchases in both good times and bad and the price at which the shares are sold is more than their average cost. (*See* Formula Investing)

DOUBLE EXEMPTION   Refers to securities that are exempt from state as well as federal income taxes.

DOUBLE TAXATION   Short for double taxation of dividends. The federal government taxes corporate profits once as corporate income; any part of the remaining profits distributed to stockholders may be taxed again as income to the recipient stockholder.

DOW THEORY   A theory of market analysis based upon the performance of the Dow Jones industrial and transportation stock-price averages. The theory says the market is in a basic upward trend if one of these averages advances above a previous important high, accompanied or followed by a similar advance in the other. When the averages both dip below previous important lows, this is regarded as confirmation of a basic downward trend. The theory does not attempt to predict how long either trend will continue, although it is widely misinterpreted as a method of forecasting future action.

Down-Tick   (*See* Up-Tick)

Earnings Report   A statement—also called an income statement—issued by a company showing its earnings or losses over a given period. The earnings report lists the income earned, expenses, and the net result. (*See* Balance Sheet)

Equipment Trust Certificate   A type of security, generally issued by a railroad, to pay for new equipment. Title to the equipment, such as a locomotive, is held by a trustee until the notes are paid off. An equipment trust certificate is usually secured by a first claim on the equipment.

Equity   The ownership interest of common and preferred stockholders in a company. Also refers to excess of value of securities over the debit balance in a margin account.

Exchange Acquisition   A method of filling an order to buy a large block of stock on the floor of an exchange. Under certain circumstances, a member-broker can facilitate the sale of a block of stock by soliciting and getting other member-brokers to solicit orders to buy. Individual buy orders are lumped together and crossed with the sell order in the regular auction market. A special commission is usually paid by the seller; ordinarily the buyer pays no commission.

Ex-Dividend   A synonym for "without dividend." The buyer of a stock selling ex-dividend does not receive the recently declared dividend. Every dividend is payable on a fixed date to sell shareholders recorded on the books of the company as of a previous date of record. For example, a dividend may be declared as payable to holders of record on the books of the company on a given Friday. Since five business days are allowed for delivery of stock in a "regular-way" transaction on the New York Stock Exchange, the Exchange would declare the stock "ex-dividend" as of the opening of the market on the preceding Monday. That means anyone who bought it after Monday would not be entitled to that dividend. When stocks go ex-dividend, the stock tables include the symbol "A" following the name. (*See* Cash Sale; Net Change; Transfer)

Ex-Rights   Without the rights, corporations raising additional money may do so by offering their stockholders the right to subscribe to new or additional stock, usually at a discount from the prevailing market price. The buyer of a stock selling ex-rights is not entitled to the rights. (*See* Ex-Dividend; Rights)

Extra   The short form of "extra dividend." A dividend in the form of stock or cash in addition to the regular or usual dividend the company has been paying.

Face Value   The value of a bond that appears on the bond, unless the value is otherwise specified by the issuing company. Face value is ordinarily the amount the issuing company promises to pay at maturity. Face value is not an indication of market value. Sometimes referred to as par value. (*See* Par)

Fiscal Year   A corporation's accounting year. Due to the nature of their particular business, some companies do not use the calendar year for their bookkeeping. A typical example is the department store that finds December 31 too early a date to close its books after the Christmas rush. For that reason, many stores wind up their accounting year January 31. Their fiscal year, therefore, runs from February 1 of one year through January 31 of the next. The fiscal year of other companies may run from July 1 through the following June 30. Most companies, though, operate on a calendar-year basis.

FIXED CHARGES A company's fixed expenses, such as bond interest, that it has agreed to pay whether or not earned, and which are deducted from income before earnings on equity capital are computed.

FLAT The price at which a bond is traded, including consideration for all unpaid accruals of interest. Bonds in default of interest or principal are traded flat. Income bonds, which pay interest only to the extent earned, are usually traded flat. All other bonds are usually dealt in "and interest," which means that the buyer pays to the seller the market price plus interest accrued since the last payment date. When applied to a stock loan, flat means without premium or interest.

FLOOR The huge trading area—about two-thirds the size of a football field—where stocks and bonds are bought and sold on the New York Stock Exchange.

FLOOR BROKER A member of the Stock Exchange who executes orders on the floor of the Exchange to buy or sell any listed securities. (*See* Commission Broker; Two-Dollar Broker)

FORMULA INVESTING An investment technique. One formula calls for the shifting of funds from common shares to preferred shares or bonds as the market, on average, rises above a certain predetermined point—and the return of funds to common share investments as the market average declines. (*See* Dollar Cost Averaging)

FREE AND OPEN MARKET   A market in which supply and demand are freely expressed in terms of price. Contrasts with a controlled market in which supply, demand, and price may all be regulated.

FUNDAMENTAL RESEARCH   Analysis of industries and companies based on such factors as sales, assets, earnings, products or services, markets, and management. As applied to the economy, fundamental research includes consideration of gross national product, interest rates, unemployment, inventories, savings, etc. (*See* Technical Research)

FUNDED DEBT   Usually interest-bearing bonds or debentures of a company. Could include long-term bank loans. Does not include short-term loans or preferred or common stock.

GENERAL MORTGAGE BOND   A bond that is secured by a blanket mortgage on the company's property, but that may be outranked by one or more other mortgages.

GENERAL OBLIGATION BOND   A bond secured by pledge of the issuer's full faith, credit, and taxing power.

GILT-EDGED   High-grade issues by a company that has demonstrated its ability to earn a comfortable profit over a period of years and pay its bondholders their interest without interruption.

GIVE UP   A term with many different meanings. For one, a member of an exchange on the floor may act for a second member by executing an order for him with a third member. The first member tells the third member that he is acting on behalf of the second member and "gives up" the second member's name rather than his own. For another, if you have an account with Doe & Company but you're in a town where Doe has no office, you go to another member firm and tell them you have an account with Doe & Company and would like to buy some stock. After verifying your account with Doe & Company, the firm may execute your order and tell the broker who sells the stock that the firm is acting on behalf of Doe & Company. They give up the name of Doe & Company to the selling broker. Or the firm may simply wire your order to Doe & Company, who will execute it for you. The term "give up" has also been applied to a variety of other arrangements, most of which are no longer permitted.

GOOD DELIVERY   Certain basic qualifications must be met before a security sold on an exchange may be delivered. The security must be in proper form to comply with the contract of sale and to transfer title to the purchaser.

GOOD 'TIL CANCELED ORDER (GTC) OR OPEN ORDER   An order to buy or sell which remains in effect until it is either executed or canceled.

GOVERNMENT BONDS   Obligations of the U.S. Government, regarded as the highest-grade issues in existence.

GROWTH STOCK   Stock of a company with a record of growth in earnings at a relatively high rate.

GUARANTEED BOND   A bond with interest or principal, or both, guaranteed by a company other than the issuer. Usually found in the railroad industry when large roads, leasing sections of trackage owned by small railroads, may guarantee the bonds of the smaller road.

GUARANTEED STOCK   Usually preferred stock on which dividends are guaranteed by another company, under much the same circumstances as a bond is guaranteed.

HEDGE   (*See* Puts and Calls; Short Sale)

HOLDING COMPANY   A corporation that owns the securities of another, in most cases with voting control.

HYPOTHECATION   The pledging of securities as collateral— for example, to secure the debit balance in a margin account.

INACTIVE STOCK   An issue traded on an exchange or in the over-the-counter market in which there is a relatively low volume of transactions. Volume may be no more than a few hundred shares a week or even less. On the New York Stock Exchange many inactive stocks are traded in 10-share units rather than the customary 100. (*See* Round Lot)

IN-AND-OUT   Purchase and sale of the same security within a short period—a day, week, even a month. An in-and-out trader is generally more interested in day-to-day price fluctuations than dividends or long-term growth.

INCOME BOND   Generally, income bonds promise to repay principal but to pay interest only when earned. In some, unpaid interest on an income bond may accumulate as a claim against the corporation when the bond becomes due. An income bond may also be issued in lieu of preferred stock.

INDENTURE   A written agreement under which bonds and debentures are issued, setting forth maturity date, interest rate, and other terms.

INDEX   A statistical yardstick expressed in terms of percentages of a base year or years. For instance, the Federal Reserve Board's index of industrial production is based on 1967 as 100. In May 1974 the index stood at 125.4, which meant that industrial production that month was about 25 percent higher than in the base period. An index is not an average. (*See* Dollar Cost Averaging; NYSE Common)

INDUSTRIAL REVENUE BOND   A security backed by private enterprises that have been financed by a municipal issue.

INSTITUTIONAL INVESTOR   An organization whose primary purpose is to invest its own assets or those held in trust by it for others. Includes pension funds, investment companies, insurance companies, universities, and banks. At the end of 1973, institutions held approximately $226 billion in stock listed on the New York Stock Exchange, which constituted more than 31 percent of the total outstanding.

INTEREST   Payments a borrower pays a lender for the use of his money. A corporation pays interest on its bonds to its bondholders. (*See* Bond; Dividend)

INTEREST RATE   The interest payable each year, expressed as a percentage of the principal.

INVESTMENT   The use of money for the purpose of making more money, to gain income or increase capital, or both. Safety of principal is an important consideration. (*See* Speculation)

INVESTMENT BANKER   Also known as an underwriter. He is the middleman between the corporation issuing new securities and the public. The usual practice is for one or more investment bankers to buy outright from a corporation a new issue of stocks or bonds. The group forms a syndicate to sell the securities to individuals and institutions. Investment bankers also distribute very large blocks of stocks or bonds—perhaps held by an estate. Thereafter the market in the security may be over-the-counter, on a regional stock exchange, the American Exchange, or the New York Stock Exchange. (*See* Over-the-Counter; Primary Distribution; Syndicate)

INVESTMENT COUNSEL   One whose principal business consists of acting as investment adviser and a substantial part of whose business consists of rendering investment supervisory services.

INVESTOR   An individual whose principal concerns in the purchase of a security are regular dividend income, safety of the original investment, and, if possible, capital appreciation. (*See* Speculator)

ISSUE   Any of a company's securities, or the act of distributing such securities.

LEGAL LIST   A list of investments selected by various states in which certain institutions and fiduciaries, such as insurance companies and banks, may invest. Legal lists are often restricted to high-quality securities meeting certain specifications. (*See* Prudent-Man Rule)

LEVERAGE   The effect on the per-share earnings of the common stock of a company when large sums must be paid for bond interest or preferred stock dividends, or both, before the common stock is entitled to share in earnings. Leverage may be advantageous for the common when earnings are good, but may work against the common stock when earnings decline.

Example: Company A has 1 million shares of common stock outstanding and no other securities. Earnings drop from $1 million to $800,000 or from $1 to 80 cents a share, a decline of 20 percent.

Company B also has 1 million shares of common, but must pay $500,000 annually in bond interest. If earnings amount to $1 million, there is $500,000 available for the common, or 50 cents a share. But earnings drop to $800,000, so there is only $300,000 available for the common, or 30 cents a share—a drop of 40 percent. Or suppose earnings of the company with only common stock increased from $1 million to $1.5 million. Earnings per share would go from $1 to $1.50, or an increase of 50 percent.

But if earnings of the company that had to pay $500,000 in bond interest increased that much, earnings per common share would jump from 50 cents to $1 per share, or 100 percent. When a company has common stock only, no leverage exists because all earnings are available for the common, although relatively large fixed charges payable for lease of substantial plant assets may have an effect similar to that of a bond issue.

LIABILITIES   All the claims against a corporation. Liabilities include accounts and wages and salaries payable, dividends declared payable, accrued taxes payable, fixed- or long-term liabilities such as mortgage bonds, debentures, and bank loans. (*See* Balance Sheet)

LIEN   A claim against property that has been pledged or mortgaged to secure the performance of an obligation. A bond is usually secured by a lien against specified property of a company. (*See* Bond)

LIMIT, LIMITED OR LIMITED-PRICE ORDER   An order to buy or sell a stated amount of a security at a specified price, or at a better price, if obtainable after the order is represented in the Trading Crowd.

LIMITED-TAX BONDS   A bond secured by a pledge of a tax or group of taxes, limited as to rate or amount.

LIQUIDITY   The ability of the market in a particular security to absorb a reasonable amount of buying or selling at reasonable price changes. Liquidity is one of the most important characteristics of a good market.

LISTED STOCK   The stock of a company traded on a securities exchange and for which a listing application and a registration statement, giving detailed information about the company and its operations, have been filed with the Securities & Exchange Commission, unless otherwise exempted, and the exchange itself. The various stock exchanges have different standards for listing. Some of the guides used by the New York Stock Exchange for an original listing are national interest in the company, a minimum of 1 million shares publicly held among not less than 2,000 round-lot stockholders. The publicly held common shares should have a minimum aggregate market value of $16 million. The company should have net income in the latest year of over $2.5 million before federal income tax and $2 million in each of the preceding two years.

LOAD   The portion of the offering price of shares of open-end investment companies that covers sales commissions and all other costs of distributions. The load is usually incurred only on purchase, there being, in most cases, no charge when the shares are sold (redeemed).

LOCKED IN   An investor is said to be locked in when he has a profit on a security he owns but does not sell because his profit would immediately become subject to the capital-gains tax. (*See* Capital Gain)

LONG   Signifies ownership of securities. "I am long 100 U.S. Steel" means the speaker owns 100 shares. (*See* Short Position; Short Sale)

MANAGEMENT   The Board of Directors, elected by the stockholders, and the officers of the corporation, appointed by the Board of Directors.

MANIPULATION   An illegal operation. Buying or selling a security for the purpose of creating false or misleading appearance of active trading or for the purpose of raising or depressing the price to induce purchase or sale by others.

MARGIN   The amount paid by the customer when he uses his broker's credit to buy a security. Under Federal Reserve regulations, the initial margin required in the past twenty years has ranged from 50 percent of the purchase price all the way to 100 percent. (*See* Brokers' Loans; Equity; Margin Call)

MARGIN CALL   A demand upon a customer to put up money or securities with the broker. The call is made when a purchase is made, or if a customer's equity in a margin account declines below a minimum standard set by the exchange or by the firm. (*See* Margin)

MARKET ORDER   An order to buy or sell a stated amount of a security at the most advantageous price obtainable after the order is represented in the Trading Crowd. (*See* Good 'Till Canceled Order; Limit Order; Stop Order)

MARKET PRICE   In the case of a security, market price is usually considered the last reported price at which the stock or bond sold.

MARKETABILITY   The measure of ease with which a bond can be sold in the secondary market.

MATCHED AND LOST   When two bids to buy the same stock are made on the trading floor simultaneously, and each bid is equal to or larger than the amount of stock offered, both bids are considered to be on an equal basis. So the two bidders flip a coin to decide who buys the stock. Also applies to offers to sell.

MATURITY   The date on which a loan or a bond or a debenture comes due and is to be paid off.

MEMBER CORPORATION   A securities brokerage firm, organized as a corporation, with at least one member of the New York or American Stock Exchange who is director and a holder of voting stock in the corporation. (*See* Member Firm)

MEMBER FIRM   A securities brokerage firm organized as a partnership and having at least one general partner who is a member of the New York Stock Exchange. (*See* Member Corporation)

MEMBER ORGANIZATION   This term includes all New York and American Stock Exchange member firms and member corporations. The term "participant" when used with reference to a member organization includes general and limited partners of a member firm and holders of voting and nonvoting stock in a member corporation. (*See* Member Corporation; Member Firm)

MIP   Monthly Investment Plan. A pay-as-you-go method of buying odd lots of New York Stock Exchange–listed shares on a regular payment plan for as little as $40 a month or every three months and up to $1,000 per payment. Under MIP the investor buys stock by the dollars' worth—if the price advances, he gets fewer shares, and if it declines, he gets more shares. He may discontinue purchases at any time without penalty. (*See* Dollar Cost Averaging; Odd Lot)

MORAL OBLIGATION   Pledge of a legislature to assist the municipality in maintaining its debt-service requirements. In almost all instances these contractual commitments are not binding upon a future legislature.

MORTGAGE BOND   A bond secured by a mortgage on a property. The value of the property may or may not equal the value of the so-called mortgage bonds issued against it. (*See* Bond; Debenture)

MUNICIPAL BOND   A bond issued by a state or a political subdivision such as a county, city, town, or village. The term also designates bonds issued by state agencies and authorities. In general, interest paid on municipal bonds is exempt from federal income taxes and state and local income taxes within the state of issue.

NASD   The National Association of Securities Dealers, Inc. An association of brokers and dealers in the over-the-counter securities business. The Association has the power to expel members who have been declared guilty of unethical practices. NASD is dedicated to—among other objectives—"Adopt, administer and enforce rules of fair practice and rules to prevent fraudulent and manipulative acts and practices, and in general to promote just and equitable principles of trade for the protection of investors."

NASDAQ   An automated information network providing brokers and dealers with price quotations on securities traded over-the-counter. NASDAQ is an acronym for National Association of Securities Dealers Automated Quotations.

NEGOTIATED   Refers to a security, title to which is transferable by delivery. (*See* Good Delivery)

NET ASSET VALUE   A term usually used in connection with investment companies, meaning net asset value per share. It is common practice for an investment company to compute its assets daily, or even twice daily, by totaling the market value of all securities owned. All liabilities are deducted, and the balance divided by the number of shares outstanding. The resulting figure is the net asset value per share.

NET CHANGE   The change in the price of a security from the closing price on one day and the closing price on the following day on which the stock is traded. The net change is ordinarily the last figure on the stock price list. The mark +1⅛ means up $1.125 a share from the last sale on the previous day the stock traded.

NET DEBT   Gross debt less sinking-fund accumulations and all self-supporting debt.

NEW HOUSING AUTHORITY BONDS   A bond issued by a local public-housing authority to finance public housing. It is backed by the solemn pledge of the U.S. Government to see that payment is made in full.

NEW ISSUE   A stock or bond sold by a corporation for the first time. Proceeds may be issued to retire outstanding securities of the company, for new plant or equipment, or for additional working capital.

NONCUMULATIVE   A preferred stock on which unpaid dividends do not accrue. Omitted dividends are, as a rule, gone forever. (*See* Cumulative Preferred)

NYSE COMMON   A composite index covering price movements of all common stocks listed on the ''Big Board.'' It is based on the close of the market December 31, 1965 as 50.00 and is weighted according to the number of shares listed for each issue. The index is computed continuously and printed on the ticker tape each half hour. Point changes in the index are converted to dollars and cents so as to provide a meaningful measure of changes in the average price of listed stocks. The composite index is supplemented by separate indexes for four industry groups: industrials, transportation, utilities, and finances.

ODD LOT   An amount of stock less than the established 100-share unit or 10-share unit of trading: from 1 to 99 shares for the great majority of issues, and 1 to 9 for so-called inactive stocks. Odd-lot prices are geared to the auction market. On an odd-lot market order, the odd-lot dealer's price is based on the first round-lot transaction that occurs on the floor following receipt at the trading post of the odd-lot order. The differential between the odd-lot price and the ''effective'' round-lot price is 12½ cents a share. For example: You decide to buy 20 shares of ABC common at the market. Your order is transmitted by your commission broker to the representative of an odd-lot dealer at the post where ABC is traded. A few minutes later there is a 100-share transaction in ABC at $50 a share. The odd-lot price at which your order is immediately filled by the odd-lot dealer is $50.125 a share. If you had sold 20 shares of ABC, you would have received $49.875 a share. (*See* Inactive Stock; Round Lot)

ODD-LOT DEALER   A member firm of the Exchange which buys and sells odd lots of stocks—1 to 9 shares in the case of stocks traded in 10-share units and 1 to 99 shares for 100-share units. The odd-lot dealer's customers are commission brokers acting on behalf of their customers. (*See* Commission Broker; Dealer)

OFF-BOARD   This term may refer to transactions over-the-counter in unlisted securities, or to a transaction involving listed shares that was not executed on a national securities exchange. (*See* Over-the-Counter; Secondary Distribution)

OFFER   The price at which a person is ready to sell. Opposed to bid, the price at which one is ready to buy. (*See* Bid and Asked)

OPEN ORDER   (*See* Good 'Til Canceled Order)

OPTION   A right to buy (call) or sell (put) a fixed amount of a given stock at a specified price within a limited period of time. The purchaser hopes that the stock's price will go up (if he bought a call) or down (if he bought a put) by an amount sufficient to provide a profit greater than the cost of the contract and the commission and other fees required to exercise the contract. If the stock price holds steady or moves in the opposite direction, the price paid for the option is lost entirely. There are several other types of options available to the public, but these are basically combinations of puts and calls. Individuals may write (sell) as well as purchase options and are thereby obliged to deliver or buy the stock at the specified price.

When a put or call contract is purchased in the over-the-counter option market, the price at which it can be exercised is usually close to the market value at that time and is fixed for the length of the contract, which is stated in days or months and is rarely longer than a year. Six months and ten days is the most common term.

There is also a listed call-option market, which was established recently by the Chicago Board of Trade. This differs from the over-the-counter market in that trading is limited to thirty-two popular stocks, expiration of contracts is standardized at four dates during the year, exercise prices are set at multiples of 5, and option prices are determined through a continuous competitive auction market system.

ORDERS GOOD UNTIL A SPECIFIED TIME   A market or limited price order to be represented in the Trading Crowd until a specified time, after which such order or the portion thereof not executed is to be treated as canceled.

OVERBOUGHT   An opinion as to price levels. May refer to a security that has had a sharp rise or to the market as a whole after a period of vigorous buying that, it may be argued, has left prices "too high."

OVERSOLD   The reverse of overbought. A single security or a market that, it is believed, has declined to an unreasonable level.

OVER-THE-COUNTER   A market for securities made up of securities dealers who may or may not be members of a securities exchange. Over-the-counter is mainly a market made over the telephone. Thousands of companies have too few shares outstanding, not enough stockholders, and insufficient earnings to warrant application for listing on the New York Stock Exchange. Securities of these companies are traded in the over-the-counter market between dealers who act either as principals or as brokers for customers. The over-the-counter market is the principal market for U.S. Government and municipal bonds. (*See* NASD; NASDAQ; Off-Board)

PAPER PROFIT   An unrealized profit on a security still held. Paper profits become realized profits only when the security is sold. (*See* Profit-Taking)

PAR   In the case of a common share, par means a dollar amount assigned to the share by the company's charter. Par value may also be used to compute the dollar amount of the common shares on the balance sheet. Par value has little significance so far as market value of common stock is concerned. Many companies today issue no-par stock but give a stated per-share value on the balance sheet. In the case of preferred shares and bonds, however, par is important. It often signifies the dollar value upon which dividends on preferred stocks, and interest on bonds, are figured. The issuer of a 6-percent bond promises to pay that percentage of the bond's par value annually. (*See* Capitalization; Transfer Tax)

PARTICIPATING PREFERRED   A preferred stock entitled to its stated dividend and, also, to additional dividends on a specified basis upon payment of dividends on the common stock.

PASSED DIVIDEND   Omission of a regular or scheduled dividend.

PENNY STOCKS   Low-priced issues, often speculative, selling at less than $1 a share. Frequently used as a term of disparagement, although a few penny stocks have developed into investment-caliber issues.

PERCENTAGE ORDER   A market or limited-price order to buy (or sell) a stated amount of a specified stock after a fixed number of shares of such stock have traded.

POINT   In the case of shares of stock, a point means $1. If ABC shares rise 3 points, each share has risen $3. In the case of bonds, a point means $10, since a bond is quoted as a percentage of $1,000. A bond that rises 3 points gains 3 percent of $1,000, or $30 in value. An advance from 87 to 90 means an advance in dollar value from $870 to $900 for each $1,000 bond. In the case of market averages, the word point means merely that and no more. If, for example, the Dow-Jones Industrial Average rises from 870.25 to 871.25, it has risen a point. A point in this average, however, is not equivalent to $1. (See Dollar Cost Averaging)

PORTFOLIO   Holdings of securities by an individual or institution. A portfolio may contain bonds, preferred stocks, and common stocks of various types of enterprises.

PREFERRED STOCK   A class of stock with a claim on the company's earnings before payment may be made on the common stock and usually entitled to priority over common stock if the company liquidates. Usually entitled to dividends at a specified rate when declared by the Board of Directors and before payment of a dividend on the common stock—depending upon the terms of the issue. (*See* Cumulative Preferred; Participating Preferred)

PREMIUM   The amount by which a preferred stock or bond may sell above its par value. In the case of a new issue of bonds or stocks, premium is the amount the market price rises over the original selling price. Also refers to a charge sometimes made when a stock is borrowed to make delivery on a short sale. May refer, also, to redemption price of a bond or preferred stock if it is higher than face value. (*See* Discount; Short Sale)

PRICE—EARNINGS RATIO   The price of a share of stock divided by earnings per share for a twelve-month period. For example, a stock selling for $50 a share and earning $5 a share is said to be selling at a price—earnings ratio of 10 to 1.

PRIMARY DISTRIBUTION   Also called primary offering. The original sale of a company's securities. (*See* Investment Banker; Secondary Distribution)

PRINCIPAL   The person for whom a broker executes an order, or a dealer buying or selling for his own account. The term "principal" may also refer to a person's capital or to the face amount of a bond.

PROFIT-TAKING   Selling stock that has appreciated in value since purchase to realize the profit that has been made possible. The term is often used to explain a downturn in the market following a period of rising prices. (*See* Paper Profit)

PROXY   Written authorization given by a shareholder to someone else to represent him and vote his shares at a shareholders' meeting.

PRUDENT-MAN RULE   An investment standard. In some states, the law requires that a fiduciary, such as a trustee, may invest the fund's money only in a list of securities designated by the state—the so-called legal list. In other states, the trustee may invest in a security if it is one that a prudent man of discretion and intelligence who is seeking a reasonable income and preservation of capital would buy.

PUTS AND CALLS   (*See* Option)

QUOTATION   Often shortened to "quote." The highest bid to buy and the lowest offer to sell a security in a given market at a given time. If you ask your broker for a "quote" on a stock, he may come back with something like "45¼ to 45½." This means that $45.25 is the highest price any buyer wanted to pay at the time the quote was given on the floor of an exchange and that $45.50 was the lowest price that any seller would take at the same time. (*See* Bid and Asked)

RALLY   A brisk rise following a decline in the general price level of the market or in an individual stock.

RATINGS   Designations used by investors' services to give relative indications of quality; i.e., Moody's ratings from the highest, Aaa, down through Aa, A, Baa, B, etc.

RECORD DATE   The date on which you must be registered as a shareholder on the stock book of a company in order to receive a declared dividend or, among other things, to vote on company affairs. (*See* Ex-Dividend; Transfer)

REDEMPTION PRICE   The price for which a bond may be redeemed before maturity, at the option of the issuing company. Redemption value also applies to the price the company must pay to call in certain types of preferred stock. (*See* Callable)

REIT   Real Estate Investment Trust, an organization similar to an investment company in some respects but concentrating its holdings in real estate investments. The yield is generally liberal, since REITs are required to distribute as much as 90 percent of their income.

REFINANCING   Same as refunding. New securities are sold by a company and the money is used to retire existing securities. Object may be to save interest costs, extend the maturity of the loan, or both.

REGISTERED BOND   A bond which is registered on the books of the issuing company in the name of the owner. It can be transferred only when endorsed by the registered owner. (*See* Bearer Bond; Coupon Bond)

REGISTERED REPRESENTATIVE   Present name for the older term "customers' man." In a New York Stock Exchange member organization, a registered representative is a full-time employee who has met the requirements of the Exchange as to background and knowledge of the securities business. Also known as an account executive or customer's broker.

REGISTERED TRADER   A member of the Exchange who trades in stocks on the floor for an account in which he has an interest.

REGISTRAR   Usually a trust company or bank charged with the responsibility of preventing the issuance of more stock than authorized by a company.

Before a public offering may be made of new securities

by a company, or of outstanding securities by controlling stockholders—through the mails or in interstate commerce—the securities must be registered under the Securities Act of 1933. A registration statement is filed with the SEC by the issuer. It must disclose pertinent information relating to the company's operations, securities, management, and purpose of the public offering. Securities of railroads under jurisdiction of the Interstate Commerce Commission, and certain other types of securities, are exempted. On security offerings involving less than $300,000, less information is required. (*See* Transfer)

REGISTRATION   Before a security may be admitted to dealings on a national securities exchange, it must be registered under the Securities Exchange Act of 1934. The application for registration must be filed with the exchange and the SEC by the company issuing the securities. It must disclose pertinent information relating to the company's operations, securities, and management.

REGULATION T   The federal regulation governing the amount of credit that may be advanced by brokers and dealers to customers for the purchase of securities. (*See* Margin)

RETURN   (*See* Yield)

REVENUE BOND   A bond payable from revenues secured from a project that pays its way by charging rentals to the users, such as toll bridges or toll highways, or from revenues from another source which are used for a public purpose.

RIGHTS   When a company wants to raise more funds by issuing additional securities, it may give its stockholders the opportunity, ahead of others, to buy the new securities in proportion to the number of shares each owns. The piece of paper evidencing this privilege is called a right. Because the additional stock is usually offered to stockholders below the current market price, rights ordinarily have a market value of their own and are actively traded. In most cases they must be exercised within a relatively short period. Failure to exercise or sell rights may result in actual loss to the holder. (*See* Warrant)

ROUND LOT   A unit of trading or a multiple thereof. On the NYSE the units of trading are generally 100 shares in stocks and $1,000 par value in the case of bonds. In some inactive stocks, the unit of trading is 10 shares.

SCALE ORDER   An order to buy (or sell) a security that specifies the total amount to be bought (or sold) and the amount to be bought (or sold) at specified price variations.

SEAT   A traditional figure of speech for a membership on an exchange. Price and admission requirements vary.

SEC   The Securities and Exchange Commission, established by Congress to help protect investors. The SEC administers the Securities Act of 1933, the Securities Exchange Act of 1934, the Trust Indenture Act, the Investment Company Act, the Investment Advisers Act, and the Public Utility Holding Company Act.

SECONDARY DISTRIBUTION   Also known as a secondary offering. The redistribution of a block of stock some time after it has been sold by the issuing company. The sale is handed off the NYSE by a securities firm or group of firms and the shares are usually offered at a fixed price, which is related to the current market price of the stock. Usually the block is a large one, such as might be involved in the settlement of an estate. The security may be listed or unlisted. (*See* Investment Banker; Primary Distribution; Special Offering; Syndicate)

SELLERS' OPTION   A special transaction on NYSE giving the seller the right to deliver the stock or bond at any time within a specified period, ranging from not less than six business days to not more than sixty days.

SERIAL BOND   An issue that matures in relatively small amounts at periodic stated intervals.

SHORT COVERING   Buying stock to return stock previously borrowed to make delivery on a short sale.

SHORT POSITION   Stocks sold short and not covered as of a particular date. On the NYSE, a tabulation is issued once a month listing all issues on the Exchange in which there was a short position of 5,000 or more shares and issues in which the short position had changed by 2,000 or more shares in the preceding month. Short position also means the total amount of stock an individual has sold short and has not covered, as of a particular date.

SHORT SALE   A person who believes a stock will decline and sells it though he does not own any has made a short sale. For instance: You instruct your broker to sell short 100 shares of ABC. Your broker borrows the stock so he can deliver the 100 shares to the buyer. The money value of the shares borrowed is deposited by your broker with the lender. Sooner or later you must cover your short sale by buying the same amount of stock you borrowed for return to the lender. If you are able to buy

ABC at a lower price than you sold it for, your profit is the difference between the two prices—not counting commissions and taxes. But if you have to pay more for the stock than the price you received, that is the amount of your loss. Stock-exchange and federal regulations govern and limit the conditions under which a short sale may be made on a national securities exchange. Sometimes a person will sell short a stock he already owns in order to protect a paper profit. This is known as selling against the box. (*See* Up-Tick)

SIAC   Securities Industry Automation Corporation, an independent organization established by the New York and American Stock Exchanges as a jointly owned subsidiary to provide automation, data processing, clearing, and communications services.

SINKING FUND   Money regularly set aside by a company to redeem its bonds, debentures, or preferred stock from time to time as specified in the indenture or charter.

SIPC   Securities Investor Protection Corporation. Provides funds for use, if necessary, to protect customers' cash and securities, which may be on deposit with an SIPC member firm in the event the firm fails and is liquidated under the provisions of the SIPC Act. Protection is limited to $50,000 per customer account, of which no more than $20,000 may be used for cash claims. SIPC is not a government agency. It is a nonprofit membership corporation created, however, by an act of Congress.

SPECIAL BID   A method of filling an order to buy a large block on the floor of the New York Stock Exchange. In a special bid, the bidder for the block of stock—a pension fund, for instance—will pay a special commission to the broker who represents him in making the purchase. The seller does not pay a commission. The special bid is made on the floor of the Exchange at a fixed price, which may not be below the last sale of the security or the current bid in the regular market, whichever is higher. Member firms may sell this stock for customers directly to the buyer's broker during trading hours.

SPECIAL OFFERING   Opposite of a special bid. A notice is printed on the ticker tape announcing the stock sale at a fixed price, usually based on the last transaction in the regular auction market. If there are more buyers than stock, allotments are made. Only the seller pays the commission. (*See* Secondary Distribution)

SPECIALIST   A member of the New York Stock Exchange, Inc. who has two functions: First, to maintain an orderly market, insofar as is reasonably practicable, in the stocks in which he is registered as a specialist. In order to maintain an orderly market, the Exchange expects the specialist to buy or sell for his own account, to a reasonable degree, when there is a temporary disparity between supply and demand. Second, the specialist acts as a broker's broker. When a commission broker on the Exchange floor receives a limit order, say, to buy at $50 a stock then selling at $60, he cannot wait at the post where the stock is traded to see if the price reaches the specified level. So he leaves the order with the specialist, who will try to execute it in the market if and when the stock declines to the specified price. At all times the specialist must put his customer's interest above his own. There are about 350 specialists on the NYSE. (*See* Book; Limited Order)

SPECIALIST BLOCK PURCHASE   Purchase by a specialist for his own account of a large block of stock outside the regular exchange market. Such purchases may be made only when the sale of the block could not be made in the regular market within a reasonable time and at reasonable prices, and when the purchase by the specialist would aid him in maintaining a fair and orderly market. The specialist need not fill the orders on his book down to the purchase price.

SPECIALIST BLOCK SALE   Opposite of specialist block purchase. Permitted only under exceptional circumstances and subject to special procedures.

SPECULATION   The employment of funds by a speculator. Safety of principal is a secondary factor. (*See* Investment)

SPECULATOR   One who is willing to assume a relatively large risk in the hope of gain. His principal concern is to increase his capital rather than his dividend income. The speculator may buy and sell the same day or speculate in an enterprise which he does not expect to be profitable for years. (*See* Investor)

SPLIT   The division of the outstanding shares of a corporation into a larger number of shares. A 3-for-1 split by a company with 1 million shares outstanding results in 3 million shares outstanding. Each holder of 100 shares before the 3-for-1 split would have 300 shares, although his proportionate equity in the company would remain the same; 100 parts of 1 million are the equivalent of 300 parts of 3 million. Ordinarily, splits must be voted by directors and approved by shareholders. (*See* Stock Dividend)

STOCK AHEAD   Sometimes an investor who has entered an order to buy or sell a stock at a certain price will see transactions at that price reported on the ticker tape while his own order has not been executed. The reason is that other buy-and-sell orders at the same price came in to the specialist ahead of his and had priority. (*See* Specialist)

STOCK DIVIDEND   A dividend paid in securities rather than cash. The dividend may be additional shares of the issuing company or in shares of another company (usually a subsidiary) held by the company. (*See* Ex-Dividend; Split)

STOCKHOLDER OF RECORD   A stockholder whose name is registered on the books of the issuing corporation. (*See* Registrar)

STOP-LIMIT ORDER   A stop order that becomes a limit order after the specified stop price has been reached. (*See* Limit Order; Stop Order)

STOP ORDER   An order to buy at a price above or sell at a price below the current market. Stop-buy orders are generally used to limit loss or protect unrealized profits on a short sale. Stop-sell orders are generally used to protect unrealized profits or limit loss on a holding. A stop order becomes a market order when the stock sells at or beyond the specified price, and, thus, may not necessarily be executed at that price.

STOPPED STOCK   A service performed—in most cases by the specialist—for an order given him by a commission broker. Let's say XYZ just sold at $50 a share. Broker A comes along with an order to buy 100 shares at the market. The lowest offer is $50.50. Broker A believes he can do better for his client than $50.50, perhaps get the stock at $50.25. But he doesn't want to take a chance that he'll miss the market; that is, the next sale might be $50.50 and the following one even higher. So he asks the specialist if he will stop at 100 at ½ ($50.50). The specialist agrees. The specialist guarantees Broker A he will get 100 shares at 50½ if the stock sells at that price. In the meantime, if the specialist or Broker A succeeds in executing the order at $50.25, the stop is called off. (*See* Specialist)

STREET   The New York financial community in the Wall Street area.

STREET NAME   Securities held in the name of a broker instead of his customer's name are said to be carried in a "street name." This occurs when the securities have been bought on margin or when the customer wishes the security to be held by the broker.

SWITCH ORDER   An order for the purchase (sale) of one stock and the sale (purchase) of another stock at a stipulated price difference.

SWITCHING   Selling one security and buying another.

SYNDICATE   A group of investment bankers who together underwrite and distribute a new issue of securities or a large block of an outstanding issue. (*See* Investment Banker)

TAX-EXEMPT   Another name for a municipal bond. The interest on a municipal bond is exempt from federal income tax and usually tax-exempt in the state it is issued.

TECHNICAL RESEARCH   Analysis of the market and stocks based on supply and demand. The technician studies price movement, volume, and trends and patterns which are revealed by charting these factors, and attempts to assess the possible effect of current market action on future supply and demand for securities and individual issues. (*See* Fundamental Research)

TERM BOND   A bond of an issue which has a single maturity.

THIN MARKET   A market where there are comparatively few bids to buy or offers to sell, or both. The phrase may apply to a single security or to the entire stock market. In a thin market, price fluctuations between transactions are usually larger than when the market is liquid. A thin market in a particular stock may reflect lack of interest in that issue or a limited supply of or demand for stock in the market. (*See* Bid and Asked; Liquidity; Offer)

TICKER   The instrument that prints prices and volume of security transactions in cities and towns throughout the United States and Canada within minutes after each trade on the floor.

TIME ORDER   An order that becomes a market or limited-price order at a specified time.

TIPS   Supposedly "inside" information on corporation affairs.

TRADER   One who buys and sells for his own account for short-term profit. (*See* Investor; Speculator)

TRADING FLOOR   (*See* Floor)

TRADING MARKET   The secondary market for issued bonds.

TRADING POST   One of twenty-three locations on the floor of the New York Stock Exchange at which stocks assigned to that location are bought and sold. About seventy-five stocks are traded at each post.

TRANSFER   This term may refer to two different operations. For one, the delivery of a stock certificate from the seller's broker to the buyer's broker and legal change of ownership, normally accomplished within a few days. For another, to record the change of ownership on the books of the corporation by the transfer agent. When the purchaser's name is recorded on the books of the company, dividends, notices of meetings, proxies, financial reports, and all pertinent literature sent by the issuer to its securities holders are mailed direct to the new owner. (*See* Registrar; Street Name)

TRANSFER AGENT   A transfer agent keeps a record of the name of each registered shareowner, his or her address, and the number of shares owned, and sees that certificates presented to his office for transfer are properly canceled and new certificates issued in the name of the transferee. (*See* Registrar; Transfer)

TRANSFER TAX   A tax imposed by New York State when a security is sold or transferred from one person to another. The tax is paid by the seller. On sales by New York State residents, it ranges from 1.25 cents a share to 5 cents a share sold for $20 or more. Sales by out-of-state residents not employed in New York are taxed at reduced rates. There is no tax on transfers of bonds.

TREASURY STOCK   Stock issued by a company but later reacquired. It may be held in the company's treasury indefinitely, reissued to the public, or retired. Treasury stock receives no dividends and has no vote while held by the company.

TRUSTEE   A bank designated as the custodian of funds and official representative of bondholders.

TURNOVER   The volume of business in a security or the entire market. If turnover on the NYSE is reported at 15 million shares on a particular day, 15 million shares changed hands. Odd-lot turnover is tabulated separately and ordinarily is not included in reported volume.

TWO-DOLLAR BROKER   Members on the floor of the NYSE who execute orders for other brokers having more business at that time than they can handle themselves, or for firms who do not have their Exchange member on the floor. The term derives from the time when these independent brokers received $2 per hundred shares for executing such orders. The fee is paid by the broker and today it varies with the price of the stock. (*See* Commission Broker)

UNDERWRITER   (*See* Investment Banker)

UNLISTED   A security not listed on a stock exchange. (*See* Over-the-Counter)

UNLISTED TRADING PRIVILEGES   On some exchanges a stock may be traded at the request of a member without any prior speculation by the company itself. The company has no agreement to conform with standards of the exchange. Today admission of a stock to unlisted trading privileges requires SEC approval of an application filed by the exchange. The information in the application must be made available by the exchange to the public. No unlisted stocks are traded on the New York Stock Exchange. (*See* Listed Stock)

UP-TICK   A term used to designate a transaction made at a price higher than the preceding transaction. Also called a "plus-tick." A stock may be sold short only on an up-tick, or on a "zero-plus" tick. A zero-plus tick is a term used for a transaction at the same price as the preceding trade but higher than the preceding different price.

Conversely, a down-tick, or "minus" tick, is a term used to designate a transaction made at a price lower than the preceding trade. A "zero-minus" tick is a transaction made at the same price as the preceding sale but lower than the preceding different price.

A plus sign or a minus sign is displayed throughout the day next to the last price of each company's stock traded at each trading post on the floor of the New York Stock Exchange. (*See* Short Sale)

VOTING RIGHTS   The stockholder's right to vote his stock in the affairs of the company. Most common shares have one vote each. Preferred stock usually has the right to vote when preferred dividends are in default for a specified period. The right to vote may be delegated by the stockholder to another person. (*See* Cumulative Voting; Proxy)

WARRANT   A certificate giving the holder the right to purchase securities at a stipulated price within a specified time limit or perpetually. Sometimes a warrant is offered with securities as an inducement to buy. (*See* Rights)

WHEN ISSUED   A short form of "when, as and if issued." The term indicates a conditional transaction in a security authorized for issuance but not as yet actually issued. All "when issued" transactions are on an "if" basis, to be settled if and when the actual security is issued and the Exchange or National Association of Securities Dealers rules the transactions are to be settled.

WIRE HOUSE   A member firm of an exchange maintaining a communications network linking either its own branch offices, offices of correspondent firms, or a combination of such offices.

WORKING CONTROL   Theoretically, ownership of 51 percent of a company's voting stock is necessary to exercise control. In practice—and this is particularly true in the case of a large corporation—effective control sometimes can be exerted through ownership, individually or by a group acting in concert, of less than 50 percent.

YIELD   Also known as "return." The dividends or interest paid by a company expressed as a percentage of the current price.

INDEX

New York Times Index, 59
No-load vs. load funds, 73n, 74, 114
NOW checking accounts, 40

O

Odd lots, 55
Oil, 158–59
Omega, 114
OMNI, 114
Oppenheimer Gold and Special Minerals Fund, 135
Oppenheimer Regency Fund, 75
Option premiums, 77, 79–80
OTC Market, 51–53

P

Par, 89, 99
Penny Stock Journal, 53
Penny stocks, 53–54
Pension Benefit Guaranty Corporation, 169
Pension plans, 18, 95–96
  private, 166–68
  zero-coupon bonds used in, 197. *See also* Individual retirement accounts (IRAs); Keogh plans.
PHA bonds, 93, 97
Platinum, 131
Pouring over, 191
Preferred stocks, 50
Premium, 77, 79–80, 89
Price-earnings ratio, 58
Probate, 128
Probate estate, 182
Profit-sharing plan, 95, 170–72
Property insurance, 119
Prospectus, 74–75

Prudential, 44
Public vs. private tax shelters, 152–53, 162
Put bonds, 98–99
Put options, 23, 47, 70, 78
  purchasing, 80, 82
  selling, 83
  writing, 85–86
  writing covered calls vs. buying, 84

Q

Qualified pension plan, 167
Qualified terminable interest property (Q-tip) trust, 191

R

Rating services, 87, 90–91
Real estate, 13
  illiquidity risk associated with, 19
  and risk tolerance, 20–21
  risk vs. rewards in, 154
  as tax-sheltered investment, 156–58
Recapture, 149–50, 158
Registered vs. bearer securities, 96
Repurchase agreement (repros), 106–7
Research and development (R&D), 160
Residence information, 26
Resistance level, 69
Retirement, 5, 11, 15, 17, 21, 30, 197. *See also* Individual retirement accounts (IRAs); Social Security.

ABOUT THE AUTHOR

Gene Mackevich is First Vice President of E. F. Hutton & Company, based in the Chicago Board of Trade Office. Mackevich is the author of *The Women's Money Book: How To Make Your Money Grow*, in addition to numerous newspaper and magazine articles. He appears frequently as an investment and financial expert on radio and television talk shows, and regularly for the last seven years as the weekly business and finance adviser to the Dave Baum Radio Show in Chicago. Mackevich and his family team of financial planners—wife Barbara, son Jeffrey, and daughter Marietta—have been recognized as one of the top 20 financial planning groups in the United States and Canada by *Registered Representative* magazine, the leading industry publication. Mackevich is licensed on the NYSE and AMEX and by the National Association of Security Dealers, and holds real estate and insurance broker's licenses.